Planning Commission's

Report of the Committee on

India Vision 2020

and

vision documents of some states

Planning Commission's

Report of the Committee on

India

Vision 2020

and

vision documents of some states

ECONOMICA INDIA INFO-SERVICES
(A DIVISION OF ACADEMIC FOUNDATION)

ACADEMIC FOUNDATION
NEW DELHI

Published in 2003 by

ACADEMIC FOUNDATION
4772-73 / 23 Bharat Ram Road,
(23 Ansari Road), Darya Ganj,
New Delhi - 110 002.

Phones : 23245001, 02, 03, 04.

Fax : 011-23245005

e-mail : academic@vsnl.com

www : academicfoundation.com

India : Vision 2020
and vision documents of some states

ISBN 81-7188-302-8

Laser-Typeset at AF's DTP Division.
Printed at Print Perfect, Mayapuri, New Delhi.

Contents

India Vision : 2020

Report of the Committee on
India: Vision 2020

Chairman : S.P. Gupta

PLANNING COMMISSION, GOVERNMENT OF INDIA

(The Complete Report)

Contents

Foreword

Every country needs a vision statement which stirs the imagination and motivates all segments of society to greater effort. It is an essential step in building a political consensus on a broad national development strategy, which encompasses, inter-alia, the roles and responsibilities of different agents in the economy, such as Central, State and local government, the private corporate sector, the small and tiny sector, people's organisations etc. It must identify the potential risks and bottlenecks and their possible solutions in order to mobilise efforts in a focussed manner. It is clear, therefore, that to meet these objectives, a vision statement has to operate at several levels of generality and specificity.

In order to address these issues, among others, the Planning Commission constituted a Committee on Vision 2020 for India in June 2000 under the chairmanship of Dr. S.P. Gupta, Member, Planning Commission. This initiative brought together over 30 experts from different fields. Their deliberations, extending over a period of more than two years, has helped to throw up a range of interesting possibilities, critical issues and crucial decision-points for government and private bodies for future action.

The Report of the Committee examines many important issues, but the ones that stand out most powerfully are employment and education. In order to ensure access to food and other essentials of a healthy life for all citizens, India faces the challenge of generating 200 million new employment opportunities over the next two decades. This report calls for raising employment generation to the top of the nation's development agenda and marshalling all available resources to create employment opportunities for all job-seekers. It goes even further by identifying the sectors which offer the greatest potential for job creation as well as critical policy issues that need to be addressed in order to fully tap that potential.

Education is the second main thrust area of this document. Greater coverage and better quality education at all levels from basic literacy to hi-tech science and technology is the essential prerequisite for raising agricultural productivity and industrial quality, spurring growth of India's budding IT and biotechnology sectors, stimulating growth of manufactured and service exports, improving health and nutrition, domestic stability and quality of governance. The report calls for concerted efforts to abolish illiteracy, achieve 100 per cent enrolment at primary and secondary levels, and broaden access to higher education and vocational training through both traditional and non-traditional delivery systems.

The document also examines issues related to population growth, food production, health, vulnerable sections of the population, transport, communication, energy self-sufficiency, water conservation and air quality, trade investment, peace, security and governance. It gives projections of India in 2020 in business as usual and in the best case scenario in various important sectors and also identifies nodal points of Indian prosperity. Its central conclusion is that India has the opportunity to emerge as one of the world's leading economies over the next two decades, provided her citizens have the self-confidence, the self-reliance, the will and the determination to realise their individual and collective potentials.

The turn of a century, and most especially the beginning of a new millennium, is an appropriate time for reflecting on the unfinished tasks of nation-building and the country's future possibilities, and placing the present Tenth Plan in tune with a Vision document. I commend the Vision 2020 Committee and especially Dr. S.P. Gupta for preparing this document that will provide a framework and perspective for those in government and the private sector who are tasked with formulating initiatives for national prosperity. I hope that this document will arouse public interest and debate which will help us to refine it further in the years to come.

— K.C. Pant

Acknowledgement

The Committee on Vision 2020 had been constituted by the Planning Commission in June, 2000, under my chairmanship, for crystallising the country's vision for the future in the year 2020. The vision will reflect people's aspirations, the full potentials of growth and development, and lay out the efforts needed to fulfill this vision. The details of the terms of reference of this Committee and their composition have been given in the Annexure.

The Committee comprised more than 30 members and invitees from different walks of life, all experts in their respective areas, and they spent nearly two years to deliberate upon and assess the vision of the people by producing many notes and papers which have now become the basis of this Report. The details of most of the papers are yet to be finalised and edited. Once done, it is proposed to place them in the Planning Commission website prior to final publication, as background papers for this vision document.

I am indebted very much to all the Members of the Committee, the invitees and the many distinguished participants in all the meetings over which the Report has been deliberated. Their inputs were very valuable for designing and formulating this vision document. Besides, we also benefited from other innumerable sources covering many books, published and unpublished papers, and views and comments given by a large number of academics and policy makers. We got the benefit of several other vision 2020 documents pertaining to other countries and policies of different states in India. We have also gained from the vision of Dr. A.P.J. Abdul Kalam's book, *India 2020: A Vision for the New Millennium.*

Among the Members and invitees, we received special help in

formulating and preparing this vision from Professor Gary Jacobs, Mother's Service Society, Pondicherry, Dr. H. Ramachandran, Director, I.A.M.R., Shri Mahesh Kapoor, Dr. Manas Bhattacharrya, DDG, Department of Telecommunications, Shri R.P. Sinha, former Principal Adviser, Planning Commission, Professor Mari Bhat, Institute of Economic Growth, to mention only a few. In preparing this document, I have been helped enormously by Dr. Amit S. Ray, Member-Secretary of the Committee, and Professor Gary Jacobs and Dr. Nandita Khadria, members of the editorial group. I have also been fortunate to have very valuable inputs, help and suggestions from all the Principal Advisers and Advisers of the Planning Commission, including Shri Lakshmi Ratan, Dr. (Mrs.) Prema Ramachandran, Dr. (Mrs.) Rohini Nayyar, Mrs. T.K. Sarojini, Dr. Pronab Sen, Shri Shailendra Sharma, Mr. Rohit Sarkar, Shri A. Sekhar, Shri B.N. Puri, and Shri L.P. Sonkar, to mention only a few. My special thanks goes to all the Members of the Planning Commission for their support and advice and especially to Dr. D.N. Tewari, who helped me always whenever needed.

I wish also to place on record the excellent secretarial help provided by Shri Ashok Kumar Sharda, Shri P. Sankar, Shri Hemant Gaba, Ms. Neelam Khanduri and Shri P.R. Chatterjee of my office.

Before I end, I must express my respect to late Shri J.N. Maggo, who was the Member-Secretary at the outset of this project, and my thanks to Dr. Shovan Ray who later on succeeded him until he left the Planning Commission and joined IGIDR, Mumbai.

Lastly, but above all, my gratitude goes to Shri K.C. Pant, Deputy Chairman, Planning Commission, for giving me the opportunity to undertake the study reflecting the longer term perspective of the country's plan outlook amidst constant encouragement and guidance.

— S.P. Gupta

December 5, 2002

Summary and Overview

Our vision of India's future should be both comprehensive and harmonious. It must encompass all the myriad aspects that constitute the life of the country and its people. It must balance and synthesise all the divergent views and forces that compete in the pursuit of self-fulfilment. It must be based on an objective assessment of facts and a realistic appraisal of possibilities, yet it must rise beyond the limitations of past trends, immediate preoccupations and pressing challenges to perceive the emerging opportunities and concealed potentials.

Most of all, our vision of India's future should serve to awaken in all of us a greater awareness of our cultural and spiritual strengths – which formed the bedrock of our past achievements and should form the foundation of our future accomplishments. Some of our traditions must change, but knowledge, in essence, is our greatest endowment. The vision should awaken in us an unswerving confidence in ourselves, a complete reliance on our own capacity as a nation and an unshakeable determination to realise our full potential. A true vision cannot be a static written statement. It must emerge as a living a dynamic reality in the minds and hearts of the people and their leaders.

This vision statement of India 2020 may not fulfill all these criteria to our full satisfaction, but it can serve as a useful starting point and foundation for contemplating future possibilities and our destiny as a nation. It can serve to indicate the board lines of policy and strategy by which India can emerage as a far stronger, more prosperous and more equitable nation in the coming years.

This document draws upon many ideas and proposals contained in more than thirty background papers presented to the Committee over the last two years, which have been presented in the main body. The vast scope and complexity of the issues prevent us from doing full justice to them in this summary[1].

This vision statement is neither a prediction of what will actually occur, not simply a wish list of desirable but unattainable ends. Rather, it is a statement of what we belive is possible for our nation to achieve, provided we are able to fully mobilise all the available resources – human, organisational, technological and financial – generate the requisite will and make the required effort. In formulating our vision of the future India, it is important to see beyond the limits of the immediate past to rediscover the greatness that is India. Although the present Republic of India is a young developing nation, our people have a rich and illustrious history as one of the longest living civilisations in the world. In 1835, even Lord Macaulay, the British historian politician had to admit before the British Parliament: "I have travelled across the length and breadth of India and I have not seen one person who is a beggar, who is a thief. Such wealth I have seen in this country, such high moral values, people of such caliber.... the very backbone of this nation, which is her spiritual and cultural heritage...." *Thus, it would be wrong to state that in 1947 India started to construct a modern nation from scratch. Rather, it began the process of rediscovering its rich cultural and spiritual values that had formed the foundation of India in the past. It is on this foundation that we seek to formulate our vision of India 2020.*

An essential requirement for envisioning India's future in the new century is to recognise that the parameters which determine national development have changed in recent years and will change further in future. This will open up greater possibilities than ever before. A powerful set of catalytic forces is accelerating the speed of social change throughout the world. They include a rapid rise in levels of education, high rates of technological innovation and application, ever faster and cheaper communication that dissolves physical and social barriers both within countries and internationally, greater availability and easier access to information,

1. These selected papers will be placed in the website after the fully edited versions are obtained.

and the further opening up of global markets. These trends are representative of a relative shift in the engines that drive development from manufacturing to the services sector and from capital resources to human and knowledge resources. Technology, organisation, information, education and productive skills will, therefore, play a critically decisive role in governing the future course of development.

The growing influence of these factors, acting on the foundation of India's increasingly dynamic and vibrant economic base, lend credence to the view that India can achieve and sustain higher than historical rates of economic growth in the coming decades. The compounded effect of achieving the targeted annual GDP growth rate of 8.5 to 9 per cent over the next 20 years would result in a quadrupling of the real per capita income and almost eliminating the percentage of Indians living below the poverty line. This will raise India's rank from around 11th today to 4th from the top in 2020 among 207 countries given in the World Development Report in terms of GDP. Further, in terms of per capita GDP measured in ppp India's rank will rise by a minimum of 53 ranks from the present 153 to 100. This will mean, India will move from a low income country to an upper middle income country. This is a very real possibility for us to seize upon and realise.

What will India be like 20 years from now? While in some areas we can confidently estimate quantitatively the outcome with a fair degree of accuracy, in some others we only know the broad direction. In still others we are unable to say with confidence the direction that future trends will take. We can only indicate what would be most desirable and signal the opportunities and obstacles that will arise along the way.

By 2020, the people of India will be more numerous, better educated, healthier and more prosperous than at any time in our long history.

In spite of the declining fertility rates, falling infant mortality and increasing life expectancy will spur an increase of at least 300 million people. The result: Total population of India will exceed 1.3 billion in 2020. A marked slowdown in birth rates will leave the under-15 population at roughly the same size as it is today (i.e., increase by 0.2 per cent per annum). This means that the pressure for expansion of the educational system will come only from increasing enrolment and efforts to reduce drop-out rates. The population over 60 years of age will double from 60 to 120 million people (i.e., around 3.5 per cent per annum). This will necessitate the adoption of special measures to support this vulnerable group, which will include a high percentage of illiterates and who are especially susceptible to both malnutrition and health-related problems. Unequal rates of population and economic growth are likely to further aggravate regional disparities within the country.

Well before 2020, India will have the capacity to produce more than sufficient quantities of food to provide a healthy diet to its entire population and become a major food exporter. Even by maintaining the moderate rates of productivity growth achieved during the 1990s, the country will be able to meet the projected demand in all major food categories and generate a substantial surplus of food grains and dairy products. Rising productivity and rapid diversification into value-added crops could spur another Green Revolution in Indian agriculture.

Production of surplus food will not, however, ensure the eradication of under-nutrition. In spite of enormous progress in the food production, nearly half the country's population still suffers from chronic under-nutrition and malnutrition. The most vulnerable are children, women and the elderly among the lower income groups. Eradication of this scourge will require the generation of sufficient employment opportunities so that all households have the purchasing power needed for assured economic access to food. Employment or livelihood security is an essential and inseparable element of a comprehensive strategy for national food security. Conversely, food security is an essential requirement for raising the productivity of India's workforce to international levels.

As population growth slows to replacement levels over the next two decades, India's greatest challenge will be to provide employment opportunities for all job-seekers. The working age population will expand by about 45 per cent, spurring rapid growth of the labour force and the number of job-seekers. Major changes in economic policy and strategy will be needed to eliminate the current backlog of more than 34 million unemployed job-seekers and assure employment opportunities for all additions to the labour force. India needs to generate around 200 million additional employment opportunities over the next 20 years. At the same time, the total proportion of the workforce involved in agriculture is likely to decline from 56 per cent to 40 per cent or even lower, thus increasing the pressure for rapid multiplication of non-farm employment opportunities.

Access to gainful employment is an essential condition for citizens to exercise their economic rights in a market democracy. The capacity to pay is the economic equivalent of the right to vote. India's vision for 2020 must be founded on the premise of Jobs for All. Employment must be considered a constitutional right of every citizen, backed by the full commitment of the Government. Granted that the requisite political will is forthcoming, the goal of full employment is certainly achievable. This will require a reorientation of national priorities, technology policy and government action. Formerly separate lines of sectoral planning need to be integrated around a central vision and set of goals, of which full employment must be one.

How and in which fields will these additional job opportunities be created? There are abundant opportunities and ample means available to the nation to achieve the objective of creating additional employment opportunities. The public organised sector however cannot be the target area, since it will continue to shed jobs for quite some time. Although the growth of the private organised sector will contribute significantly to the growth of the economy, its contribution to employment generation will be quite modest, since total employment in this sector at present represents only 2.5 per cent of all jobs. The largest number of new jobs will be created by small and medium enterprises (SMEs), which contribute the vast majority of private sector jobs in more advanced economies such as the USA, Japan and Korea. International experience confirms that SMEs are better insulated from the external shocks, more resistant to the stresses, and more responsive to the demands of the fast-chaning technology adoption, globalisation and entrepreneurial development. Employment has nearly tripled in India's small and medium sector over the past 20 years. A repetition of this performance would generate an additional 150-200 million jobs by 2020. A comprehensive package of venture capital, credit, liberalisation of controls, technology, training, marketing and management measures is needed to ensure continous expansion of this sector.

The vision document identifies a number of high employment potential sectors, including commercial agriculture, agro-industry and agri-business; forestation for pulp, fuel and power; retail and wholesale trade; tourism, housing and construction; IT and IT-enabled services; transport and communications; education, health and financial services. While all these sectors are already expanding, a wide range of strategies and policies are available to stimulate more rapid development. Induction of advanced crop technology will reduce production costs and expand the market for important commercial crops. Linkages to down-stream agro-industries can dramatically reduce waste and spoilage of perishable commodities, while broadening the range of marketable products. Adoption of an agriculture-based energy policy focusing on production of fuel oil and biomass power could generate millions of additional on-farm jobs and lucrative alternative markets for farm produce, while reducing the country's dependence on imported fuels. Tourism-related occupations presently employ only 5.6 per cent of the Indian workforce, compared to 10.8 per cent globally. Development of India's tourism infrastructure, combined with modifications in air transport, hotel rates and tax policies could generate an additional 25 million employment opportunities in this sector. Outsourcing of services by OECD countries will fuel a rapid expansion of IT and IT-enabled services, generating millions of jobs within the country. The country will also require millions of additional teachers and medical professionals to meet the surging demand for education and health services.

While it is difficult to project unemployment rates 20 years into the future, rising levels of education and growth of the over-60 age group will mitigate, to some extent, the growth of the labour force. Combined with the enormous opportunities for creation of new employment opportunities, the incidence of unemployment could be almost eliminated by 2020.

Successful education policy forms the bedrock of all fields of national development — political, economic, technical, scientific, social and environmental. Education is the foundation for a vibrant democracy, growth of productivity and income and employment opportunities. Literacy must be considered the minimum right and equirement of every Indian citizen. Presently, the country has about 300 million illiterate adults. The Government's goal is to achieve 75 per cent literacy within the next five years. A 100 per cent literate India is of paramount importance for realising the greater vision presented in this document.

Literacy is an indispensable minimum condition for development, but it is far from sufficient. In this increasingly complex and technologically sophisticated world, 10 years of school education must also be considered an essential prerequisite for citizens to adapt and succeed economically, avail of social opportunities and develop their individual potentials. The current enrolment rate for primary education is around 77 per cent and for secondary education about 60 per cent. Achieving 100 per cent enrolment of all children in the 6 to 14 year age group is an ambitious but achievable goal for 2020 that should be pursued as a top priority.

Increasing enrolment to cover the entire school-age population needs to be combined with efforts to increase the quality and relevance of school curriculum to equip students with not only academic knowledge, but also values and life-knowledge. A qualitative shift is needed from routine memorisation to development of children's capacity for critical thinking and from methods that emphasise teaching and passive learning to those that foster active interest and the ability of children to learn on their own.

Concentrated efforts are needed to tap the potentials of alternative methods of knowledge delivery for both school going and non-school going children and adults, including television, computerised self-learning and Internet-based courses. Given the huge number of young students that will quest for all levels of higher education and a severe shortage of qualified instructors, and given India's outstanding expertise in the IT industry, the country should embark on a massive programme to convert progressively the higher educational curriculum into a multi-media, web-based format and to establish accredited standards for recognition of courses taught under distance education programmes.

Our vision of India in 2020 is predicated on the belief that human resources are the most important determinant of overall development. A more than doubling of investment in education from the current level of 3.2-4.4 per cent of GNP is the soundest policy for quadrupling the country's GNP per capita.

The knowledge and skill of our workforce will be a major determinant of India's future rate of economic growth as well as the type and number of jobs we create. Currently, only five per cent of the country's labour force in the 20-24 age category have undergone formal vocational training, compared to levels ranging from 28 per cent in Mexico to 96 per cent in Korea. A comprehensive strategy is needed to enhance the nation's employable skills, including a cataloging of the entire range of vocational skills required to support development, expansion of the nation's system of vocational training institutes, widening of the range of vocational skills taught, and active involvement of the private sector in skill delivery. A national network of 50,000 or more computerised vocational centres run by private self-employed businesses, similar to the STD booths and Internet cafes, can deliver low-cost, high-quality training to 10 million workers every year — more than five times the total number covered by existing programmes. A parallel effort is required to upgrade the skills of Indian farmers, who represent 56 per cent of the total workforce. The existing system of 300 Krishi Vignan Kendras needs to be expanded and supplemented by a national network consisting of thousands of farm schools offering practical demonstration and training on lands leased from farmers in the local community.

The health of a nation is a product of many factors and forces that combine and interact. Economic growth, per capita income, employment, literacy, education, age at marriage, birth rates, availability of information regarding health care and nutrition, access to safe drinking water, public and private health care infrastructure, access to preventive health and medical care, and health insurance are among the contributing factors. Measued in terms of infant mortality rates, maternal mortality, life expectancy and nutrition, the health of the Indian population has improved dramatically over the past 50 years. Yet, despite these achievements, wide disparities exist between different income groups, between rural and urban communities, between different states and even districts within states, and a big gap from the level attained by the high middle income and advanced developed country.

Communicable diseases remain the major cause of illness. During the next 5 to 10 years, existing programmes are likely to eliminate polio and leprosy and substantially reduce the prevalence of kalaazar and filariasis. However, TB, malaria and AIDS will remain major public health problems. Improved diagnostic services and treatment can reduce the prevalance and incidence of TB by 2020. Restructuring the workforce and strengthening health care infrastructure can reduce the incidence of malaria by 50 per cent or more within a decade. Childhood diarrhea, another major cause of illness, can be largely prevented through community action and public education. Childhood under-nutrition can be addressed by targeting children of low birth weight and utilising low-cost screening procedures. Given the projected improvement in living standards, food security, educational levels and access to health care among all levels of the population, dramatic progress can be achieved in reducing the prevalance of severe under-nutrition in children substantially by 2020. Although private expenditure on health care is expected to rise sharply, the level of public expenditure needs to rise about four-fold from present levels in order to support a more equitable and effective health care system, providing universal access, fair distribution of financial costs, and special attention to vulnerable groups such as women, children, the aged and disabled. Health insurance can also play an invaluable role in improving the health care system.

Literacy and general education form the base of the knowledge pyramid which is essential for a rapid and sustained development of the society in the 21st Century. The continuous advancement of science and the application of improved technology constitute the middle rung. Social ideals and values form the apex. Technical education, both vocational and professional, provide the foundation for development of science and technology. A large number of the country's engineering colleges need to be upgraded to quality standards nearer to those of India's world-class IITs. India's expenditure on R&D, which is currently 1/60th that of Korea, needs to be considerably enhanced. Another essential requirement is to improve the linkage between technology development and technology application by fostering close ties between basic research and business.

India's urban population is expected to rise from 28 per cent to 40 per cent of the total population by 2020, placing increasing strain on the country's urban infrastructure. Future growth is likely to concentrate in and around 60 to 70 large cities having a population of one million or more. Decentralisation of municipal governance and greater reliance on institutional financing and capital markets for resource mobilisation are likely to increase the disparity between the larger and smaller urban centres. A satisfying outcome will depend on the formulation of effective public policies to accelerate all-round development of smaller urban centres and to refashion the role of the state as an effective facilitator to compensate for the deficiencies of market mechanisms in the delivery of public goods.

Simultaneous efforts are needed to strengthen the rural infrastructure relating to education, health care, transport, telecom, power and water. Unless bold steps are taken to promote a geographically more dispersed and equitable development paradigm, widening disparities between rural and urban centres will accelerate the migration to cities and the rapid expansion of urban slum areas. One promising alternative approach is to link clusters of villages together by high speed circular highways, thereby bringing 100,000 or more people into a circular community that can be crossed within 30 minutes of travel time, and promoting a balanced and distributed development of urban services along the periphery of the ring road.

Rapid flow of information is a catalyst for social development. Vision 2020 conceives of India evolving into an information society and knowledge economy built on the edifice of information and communication technology (ICT), of which telecommunications is the springboard. Rapid expansion and extension of the country's fixed and mobile telecom infrastructure is essential for stimulating growth of both the ICT sector and the economy as a whole. The number of fixed telephone line services will multiply another seven-fold in the next 18 years. As the fixed line market matures, more and more users will cross over to mobile communications as well, spurring a mobile revolution in India. Mobile telecommunications and the Internet will set the contours of technological progress over the next two decades. The third generation mobile devices with access to mobile data and voice should be within reach of wide sections of the population by 2020.

Development involves a continuous increase in the number of physical transactions and the speed with which they occur, both of which are highly dependent on the size and quality of the nation's transport system. Efforts to achieve higher GDP growth rates in future years cannot be sustained without correspondingly greater efforts to strengthen the nation's transport system. Based on the projected GDP growth of 8 per cent per annum, the total freight traffic is likely to reach five times the level in 2000. Passenger traffic is expected to increase more than four-fold over the next 20 years.

Increasing population combined with continued urbanisation will fuel the explosive growth of personal vehicle movement in cities, which can only be curtailed by massive investment in mass transport services. Specific plans need to be formulated by each urban authority, starting with the provision of bus services, developing intermediate public transport and identifying corridors for future growth, including reserving land for such activity. In the long run, rail-based mass transport systems appear to be the only viable solution to the problems of urban transport in India's major metropolitan areas.

A key component for rural development is the provision of roads for connectivity, access being essential for social and economic well-being. Families residing alongside roads benefit from better health and greater educational opportunities compared to the families living in remote villages. Based on current plans, all villages with more than 500 inhabitants will be connected by all-weather roads within the next decade.

Our vision of India 2020 is of a country having a well-developed network of roads and railways, with adequate capacity to handle the growth in transport demand. The volume of road traffic will multiply about five-fold, carried on a 70,000 km. network of national highways. State highways with at least two way lanes will link most districts. Rural roads will provide access to the furthest outlying villages. Technological progress is working towards generation of vehicles that are pollution free and fuel efficient. An efficient public transport system will lead to a reduction in the population of two-wheelers in major urban areas. We also envisage that connection of several major rivers through a network of interlinking canals will provide impetus to rapid growth of low-cost, inland water transport.

Total investment requirements to meet these needs will increase to levels three to four times higher than present levels in real terms. While the government will continue to be a major source of funds for infrastructure, internal generation of resources by the transport services will have to increase, supported by more realistic pricing of transport services, reduction in operating costs, and active involvement of the private sector in the development and operation of transport systems.

Economic growth is driven by energy that powers the nation's industries, vehicles, homes and offices. For future growth to be both rapid and sustainable, the energy source needs to be as resource-efficient and environmentally benign as possible. Total demand for power is expected to increase by another 3.5 times or more in the next two decades, which will necessitate a tripling of installed generation capacity from 101,000 to 292,000 MW by 2020. 'Business as usual' will result in a spiralling cost for imported fuels and a surge in emission of environmental pollutants.

The overall growth in demand for all forms of fuel will mirror the growth in the power sector. Total coal demand will nearly double, and both oil and gas demand will triple. Expanding domestic production capacity will require substantial investments, while increasing dependence on imported forms of energy will increase vulnerability to fluctuations in global energy prices. Surging demand will also place increased burden on the physical and social environment. Enhanced adoption by the public and private sector, of best-practices and environment-friendly technologies, more efficient use of energy, promoting private sector investment, and greater efforts to protect the environment will be required to cope effectively with the nation's growing energy appetite.

Greater reliance on renewable energy sources offers enormous economic social and environmental benefits. India is already the world's fifth largest producer of wind power, with more than 95 per cent of the investment coming from the private sector. Other renewable energy technologies, including solar photovoltaic, solar thermal, small hydro, biomass power and bio-fuels are also spreading. A concerted effort to implement a more visionary approach to alternative energy generation could significantly reduce India's dependence on imported fuels while also reducing the strain on the environment. Biomass power production, ethanol motor fuel and jatropa fuel oil can generate millions of rural employment opportunities and contribute to higher rural incomes, at the same time reducing the outflow of foreign exchange. Tapping this potential will require conducive national policies and programmes designed to attract strong participation from the private sector.

India possesses 16 per cent of the world's population but just 4 per cent of its water resources. At the national level, current water resources are more than sufficient to meet the demand, but future projections show that the supply situation could become difficult over the next half century. Total water consumption is expected to rise by 20-40 per cent over the next 20 years. India is not poor in water resources. What it lacks is the ability to efficiently capture and effectively utilise the available resources for maximum benefit. The government policy needs to be revised to provide incentives for efficient use of water, including appropriate water pricing and more effective institutional mechanisms for water management. Enormous potential exists for increasing the productivity of water in agriculture by methods to raise crop productivity combined with better water management. Both urban and rural water resources can be substantially enhanced by widespread adoption of rain-water harvesting techniques, designed to capture run-off water during the monsoon season and channel it to recharge both surface water and underground aquifers. These methods need to be applied throughout the country on a massive scale, both in rural and urban areas.

Proposals to link some of the major rivers together could channel surpluses from flood-prone areas into drought-prone regions, create millions of hectares of additional irrigated land, provide an inexpensive system of inland water transport, and generate millions of additional employment opportunities in construction, agriculture, trade and industrial development. Despite the high cost of such a system, the potential benefits to the nation are so vast that pragmatic proposals demand serious consideration.

Given the vision and political will, India can convert the present water problem into a huge opportunity.

India's wide range of agro-climatic regions, vast extent of land and forest, and rich variety of biodiversity rank it among the most naturally endowed nations of the world, but its huge and still expanding human and animal populations and its urge for industrialisation tax these resources to the limit. The potential however exists for dramatically reversing the pattern of degradation that has taken place in recent decades by a systematic effort to halt soil erosion, restore precious nutrients and organic material to crop lands, recharge groundwater tables, and re-establish depleted forest lands. A combination of measures would make it possible to increase the land under forest and tree cover from the current level of 71 million hectares to 83 million hectares.

India's progress over the next 20 years will be intimately linked to events within the region and around the world. The World Bank estimates that India will become the fourth largest economy in the world by 2020. Liberalisation of trade will open up new opportunities for export of goods, while increasing pressures on domestic industry to cope with competition from imports. The global market for textiles, clothing and agricultural products will expand dramatically, but India's ability to export will depend on its capacity to keep pace with rising international standards of price, quality, productivity, and service.

The emerging global scenario will open up greater opportunities for countries with a surplus of well-educated, highly skilled labour that can provide an attractive commercial environment for the outsourcing of manufacturing and service businesses from high and even middle income countries. Export of services is a field in which India can excel. India's recent boom in outsourcing of IT services is only the tip of a rich vein of economic opportunity that could extend to a wide range of manufacturing and service businesses.

Computerisation, coupled with low cost global telecommunications are generating rapid growth of trade in service businesses, such as software and IT enabled services. This trend will accelerate, opening up vast opportunities for countries with the capacity to deliver low-cost, high-quality service. At the same time, the pressure for export of the highly educated and highly skilled individuals will also increase, so that a significant migration of scientific, engineering and medical talent is likely to continue.

Growth in the size of the international capital market will open up increasing opportunities for India to attract foreign direct and institutional investment, but a substantial improvement in infrastructure and elimination of most of the bureaucratic barriers will help India in attracting a greater share of FDI flows. Mobilisation of India's expatriate population could have momentous impact on the inflow of FDI in 2020.

India's technology policy needs to be reformulated in the light of the emerging international economic environment to capitalise on the accelerated global development and diffusion of technologies and keep pace with more demanding international standards for cost, quality and productivity. We will need to be far more aggressive in acquiring and applying advanced technologies in a wide range of fields, including agriculture, information technology, energy, health and education. At the same time, we can also aspire to become an important contributor to the expansion of global frontiers of technology by building upon and leveraging our already significant achievements in fields such as pharmaceuticals, biotechnology, software, space and energy.

India is in the midst of transforming an agrarian economy into a modern multi-dimensional economic enterprise and a traditional stratified society into an egalitarian society, while simultaneously fashioning and transforming itself into a modern democracy through consultative politics. It is inevitable that such a rapid social, economic, technological and political development of one billion people should generate turbulence. Yet it is essential that this turbulence be managed and confined within limits that preserve the social fabric and permit the nation's transformation to continue.

Underlying all our plans and hopes for a better future, underpinning all our efforts to evolve into a prosperous democratic nation is the shared aspiration of all Indian people for peace. Peace is not merely the absence or avoidance of conflict. It is the essential prerequisite for all human and social development, for which we can strive to increase our knowledge, develop our productive skills, strengthen our physical infrastructure, and integrate our multitudinous communities into a strong, united nation.

The challenges to peace are numerous and they come from all directions — from outside our borders and within, as well as from within our minds. Our capacity to preserve and build a lasting peace for all Indians will depend on the strength of our military to defend our borders, the strength of our economy to generate increasing employment and income opportunities for our citizens, the strength of our educational system to cultivate the knowledge and skills of our youth, the strength of our legal and judicial system to safeguard the rights of individuals and communities, the strength of our scientists and engineers to both develop and harness technologies for the benefit of the people, as well as the wisdom and determination of our political leaders to remove injustices and to direct the collective energies of the nation for greater achievement in every field of endeavour.

Development tends to reduce the extent of these disparities in some ways while aggravating them in others. Economic disparities aggravate perceptions of difference between sub-national, linguistic and communal groups, fostering ethnicity and communalism. A positive strategy for national security will depend on the secular and democratic values of the Indian nation deriving its strength from our culture, civilisation and freedom.

External security depends on national power. It requires a continuous enhancement of the country's capacity to use its tangible and intangible resources in such a manner as to affect the behaviour of other nations. While power is often conceived in narrow terms as military power, in the world that is emerging it must be much more broadly conceived to include political, economic, technological, social and intellectual dimensions. A vibrant economy and a leading role in international affairs may be as important as a strong military to the preservation and development of national power. Internationally, we must gravitate from a state-centered, egocentric and competitive security paradigm to a co-operative security paradigm that enhances the security of each nation by reducing potential threats to all nations. Human development in all its dimensions is and will remain our highest strategic priority.

India's economic and technological transition will be accompanied by a multifaceted political transformation that will have profound impact on the functioning of government. This transformation will foster decentralisation and devolution of power to local bodies, including financial devolution and financial responsibility; increasing direct participation of people in setting grass root priorities for distribution of resources, and building and managing local projects; and greater efficiency, transparency, and accountability in government agencies at all levels. E-governance has the potential, if fully harnessed and rightly utilised, to radically improve the speed, convenience, quality and transparency of public administrative services, while enhancing the ability of individual citizens to express and exercise their democratic rights.

Our vision of India in 2020 is of a nation bustling with energy, entrepreneurship and innovation. The country's people will be better fed, dressed and housed, taller and healthier, more educated and longer living than any generation in the country's long history. India will be much more integrated with the global economy and will be a major player in terms of trade, technology and investment. Rising levels of education, employment and incomes will help stabilise India's internal security and social environment. A united and prosperous India will be far less vulnerable to external security threats. A more prosperous India in 2020 will be characterised by a better-educated electorate and more transparent, accountable, efficient and decentralised government.

Realisation of this vision will depend on many things, but most importantly on our self-confidence, self-reliance and determination to make it a reality. For that, we need first of all to abandon the sense of dependence and the urge to imitate other nations blindly. We need also to rediscover the well-springs of our own native strength, the rich endowments of our shared culture and spiritual tradition.

We must reawaken the dormant Spirit of India.

— S.P. Gupta

1

Introduction

> A Vision is not a project report or a plan target. It is an articulation of the desired end results in broader terms.
>
> — A.P.J. Abdul Kalam

This document is neither a plan nor a projection of what India will be in 2020. Twenty years is too long a period for one or the other. Even our demographic projections, based on the most reliable data and well-documented trends, are only able to estimate the country's population two decades hence and within a range of 100 million people. How then shall we hazard a projection of the harder to measure eventualities?

The second decade of the 21st Century lies behind a barrier that is impenetrable by statistical probes. Looking backwards, we become aware of how limited our horizon of certitude really is. In the mid-1960s, when India was confronted with the threat of widespread famine and was perennially dependent on foreign food aid to feed its people, who among the most visionary of us could have imagined that within such a short period food grain production would double and the country would be having significant surpluses? Who could have anticipated the sheer speed of Japan's rise in the 1970s and 1980s or its equally surprising stagnation during the 1990s? In 1980, who could anticipate the Personal Computers revolution that was to follow just two years later? In 1983, when India's total software exports were only $12 million, who could imagine that they would multiply 500 times in 17 years and the country would be recognised around the world as a major IT power? In early 1989, who could foresee that the fall of the Berlin Wall, the end of the Cold War, the break up of the USSR and the entire Eastern Bloc would all occur within 24 months? Even a visionary like Microsoft's founder Bill Gates admits that he was unable to grasp the enormous potential of the Internet until it had already spawned a global revolution. The growth rate of our cities, which mirrors global trends of urbanisation, is 25 per cent lower today than what we predicted just five years ago.

Planning and prediction over such long time horizons as two decades are beyond our capacity, but we do possess a still greater human endowment that can enable us to envision the real possibilities and to perceive the necessary actions we need to take to convert those possibilities into realities. Call it vision or imagination, or aspiration, or anything else, it is this faculty that most differentiates us from other species and constantly drives the evolutionary progress of humanity. Vision requires a subtle blend of humility and the courage to dare.

For a vision to be realisable, it must bring into view the untapped potentials and unutilised opportunities that await exploitation both domestically and internationally, as well as the problems and challenges that impede our progress. Indeed, it is the forces which oppose our progress that generate the necessary pressure compelling us to strive harder. They may even prove to be the best indices of what will be achieved.

In envisioning a better future, we should not make the mistake of dwelling on what we lack rather than on what we possess, for India today possesses both the capacities and the opportunities to achieve a state of super-abundance. The effective strategy should focus on fully utilising the material, human, technological and social resources that we possess in the most rapid, efficient and organised manner.

A realisable vision must identify the catalytic forces that can be harnessed to accelerate the nation's development, as well as the obstacles that must be overcome, and anachronisms and out-dated attitudes done away with, in order to advance rapidly. It must frankly own past errors and troublesome propensities, but with faith in our capacity to learn from the past and change – as indeed we are now changing – with ever increasing speed. In a realisable vision, there is no room for lofty optimism based on the premise that everything will turn out for the best regardless of what we decide or how we act. But, equally, there can be no scope for extreme pessimism based on ideas that deprive us of the freedom and power to determine our own future. Our vision must express the nation's aspirations, determination and commitment for self-realisation.

We begin our visioning exercise by cataloguing the untapped potentials and under-utilised resources that are available to the nation, and then turn our attention to the present problems and emerging opportunities which constitute the raw materials from which we must fashion a better future for our country and its people.

A Vision for India

In formulating our vision of the future India, it is important to see beyond the limits of the immediate past to rediscover the greatness that is India. Although the present Republic of India is a young developing nation, our people have a rich and illustrious history as one of the longest living civilizations in the world. In 1835, even the British historian and politician, Lord Macaulay, admitted before the British Parliament: "I have travelled across the length and breadth of India and I have not seen one person who is a beggar, who is a thief. Such wealth I have seen in this country, such high moral values, people of such caliber... the very backbone of this nation, which is her spiritual and cultural heritage..."[1] Thus, it would be wrong to state that in 1947 India started to construct a modern nation from scratch. Rather, it began the process of rediscovering its rich cultural and spiritual values that had formed the foundation of India in the past. It is on this foundation that we seek to formulate our vision of India 2020.

It is indeed a challenge to formulate a cohesive vision for India in 2020. Therefore, we thought it appropriate to seek inspiration from one who had a clear vision and possessed the gift to articulate it in a manner that has inspired the hearts and minds of countless Indians. The vision articulated by Rabindranath Tagore is all encompassing in every sense. In Annexure I, we identify eight components of the vision reflected in the following poem and attempt to translate them in operational terms for India Vision 2020.

Where the mind is without fear and the head is held high.

Where knowledge is free.

Where the world has not been broken up into fragments

By narrow domestic walls.

Where words come out from the depth of truth.

Where tireless striving stretches its arms towards perfection.

Where the clear stream of reason has not lost its way

Into the dreary desert sand of dead habit.

Where the mind is led forward by Thee

Into ever-widening thought and action.

Into that heaven of freedom, my Father, let my country awake.

Rabindranath Tagore

The Challenges Ahead

India's per capita income has doubled over the past 20 years. With population growth slowing now to about 1.6 per cent per annum, a growth rate of the gross domestic product (GDP) of around 9 per cent per annum would be sufficient to quadruple the per capita income by 2020.

Opinions on achievable rates of economic growth have a tendency to swing along with the short-term economic performances. Two years ago, the global boom, the IT revolution and the all-round optimism led many to believe that in the coming decade India could mimic the 9-10 per cent growth rates that China achieved over a twenty year period. Such optimism is out of fashion today. But there is ample evidence showing that if we can adopt a longer term perspective that is not blinded by immediate circumstances and fluctuating moods, higher rates of growth should be achievable for India in the coming years. This is not a prediction — it is a potential. The reality will depend on how effectively we seize the opportunity to do so.

From a historical perspective, global rates of development have been increasing for more than a century. The dramatic rise of Japan and the East Asian tigers, and most recently China, are illustrative of this point. An objective assessment reveals that all the major engines of economic growth that have accelerated growth up till now, will be present in greater abundance in the coming years than they had been in the past.

Engines of Economic Growth

- Educational levels are rising rapidly.
- Rates of technological innovation and application are accelerating.
- Cheaper and faster communication is dissolving physical and social barriers, both within the country and internationally.
- Information is being made available in greater quantity and quality than ever before.
- Globalisation is opening up new markets.

A vision is a statement of aspirations and intentions, and therefore, it is essential that we fully recognise the need for determined effort to transform all these potentials into realities. Ultimately, it is not our capacity for prediction but our action that will determine the outcome. That action needs to be based on proper appreciation of the forces available for accelerating our progress.

Assuming that India achieves this quadrupling of per capita income by 2020, it would attain a level of development far higher than where China is today, and on par with upper-middle income countries (UMA) such as Argentina, Chile, Hungary, Malaysia, Mexico and South Africa. One day India will rise higher still, and having achieved such a target, will know HOW she achieved it. But such knowledge could be acquired even now from the experiences of the many nations that have already passed through these stages of development. From their experiences India should endeavour to acquire the underlying principles and theoretical knowledge that can then be applied appropriately to our own specific case. Therefore, we refer to the average performance of this group of UMI countries as a benchmark for our development challenges and achievable goals by 2020. Table 1 compares India's current status on some key parameters of development with the average level achieved by a group of UMI countries. It may be noted that we are not holding up the UMI countries as the goal for India in 2020, but merely using them as a reference point to indicate the magnitude of progress India needs to make in different fields. Our vision is not only to reach these reference levels but to surpass them in many cases.

Table – 1

Developmental Parameters at a Glance India Present vs. UMI Reference for India 2020

Developmental Parameters	India Present	UMI Reference for India 2020
Poverty as % of population below poverty line	26.0	13.0
Income distribution (gini index 100=equality)	37.8	48.5
Unemployment rate (% of labour force)	7.3	6.8
Male adult literacy rate (%)	68.0	96.0
Female adult literacy rate (%)	44.0	94.0
Net primary school enrolment ratio	77.2	99.9
Public expenditure on education as % GNP	3.2	4.9
Life expectancy at birth in years	64.0	69.0
Infant mortality rate per 1000 live births	71.0	22.5
Child malnutrition as % of children under 5 years based on weight for age	45.0	8.0
Public expenditure on health as % GNP	0.8	3.4
Commercial energy consumption per capita (kg of oil equiv.)	486.0	2002.0
Electric power consumption per capita (kwh)	384.0	2460.0
Telephones per 1000 population	34.0	203.0
Personal computers per 1000 population	3.3	52.3
Scientists & engineers in R&D per million population	149.0	590.0
Sectoral Composition of GDP in %		
Agriculture	28.0	6.0
Industry	26.0	34.0
Services	46.0	60.0
International trade in goods as % of ppp GDP	3.6	35.0
Foreign direct investment as % of gross capital formation	2.1	24.5
Gross FDI as % of ppp GDP	0.1	3.5

Source: Based on *World Development Indicators, 2001*, The World Bank.

Striving to achieve these reference levels and surpass them in some cases will present very significant challenges insofar as the determination and resourcefulness of the country is concerned.

Major Challenges for India

- A targeted approach to bring millions of families above the poverty line.
- Generation of nearly ten millions of new employment opportunities per annum, especially for those in the lower income groups.
- Eradication of illiteracy.
- A concerted effort to raise primary and secondary enrolment rates and minimise drop-outs.
- Improved public health to reduce infant mortality and child malnutrition.
- Massive investment in power generation, telecommunications and other physical and social infrastructure.
- Accelerated acquisition of technology capabilities to raise productivity in agriculture, industry and services.
- Becoming a more important player in the world economy in terms of both trade and investments.

We are confident that we can and will meet these challenges. We also feel that we have the knowledge and the capacity as a nation to achieve food for all, health for all, and jobs for all. What we do not know for sure however is, how long it will take us to accomplish them. We need, therefore, to affirm the will and the determination to do it rapidly and achieve it now rather than sometime later.

2

Uncommon Opportunities

Knowledge and Information Technology

An essential requirement for envisioning India's future is to recognise that the equations which determine national development have changed in recent years, opening up greater possibilities than before. The same factors continue to be at work, but their relative contribution and importance is rapidly shifting along several dimensions as shown in the figure.

Shifting Determinants of Development
Manufacturing →→ Services
Capital resources →→ Knowledge resources

The sectoral composition of the GDP changes with economic development. The predominance of agriculture in the least developed economies is reduced by the increasing importance of manufacturing, and subsequently, services, as they move up the ladder of development. As this occurs, the rates of economic growth tend to increase. This transition is now occurring globally and is reflected in the explosive growth of the services sector, especially in the fields of financial services, information and communication technology (ICT), insurance, education and health.

India's services sector has already become the dominant contributor to GDP, accounting for 46 per cent of the total, but its share is still far below the UMI reference level of 60 per cent. The country very soon will get the opportunity to skip the long slow phase of industrialisation that the most developed nations have passed through, and transit rapidly into a predominantly service economy by 2020, creating services that meet human needs, generate employment covering the large unorganised segment of the economy, raise incomes and increase purchasing power. Even our notion of services may need to evolve further to recognise the importance of the emerging knowledge-intensive services.

Knowledge has replaced capital as the most important determinant of development. In a path breaking study in mid-1950s, Nobel laureate economist Robert Solow showed that seven-eighth of the growth of US from 1900 to 1950 was accounted for by technical progress, while only one-eighth was driven by capital. A study by Denison, of factors contributing to the growth of the US economy from 1929 to 1982, attributes 94 per cent of that growth to factors relating to knowledge generation and dissemination: 64 per cent of this is linked to advances in knowledge generation (i.e. R&D) and another 30 per cent to advances in education. Better resource management, which is an application of knowledge, is also identified as a more important factor than capital. This fact bodes well for countries whose economic planners are able to escape from their earlier faith in capital and fully tap the enormous productive potential of non-material, knowledge resources.

India's Green Revolution is a dramatic example of how the input of greater knowledge in the form of improved production technologies can rapidly increase the productivity of scarce land resources. India's IT Revolution is a striking instance of how the importance of human capital has come to acquire a higher position than that of material plant and machinery.

All efforts to project India's future progress get at times blinded by the question of resources, more specifically, the financial resources needed for all plan activities. We start with the conviction that financial (capital) resources will not be the key factor that decides the course of our future progress. If we fail, it will be mainly for want of a vision of what is possible, knowledge of how to realise it, belief in ourselves, commitment to achieve, will for the effort or skill in implementation — and not for lack of finance.

The knowledge revolution is not just a short-term blip on the radar screen which peaked in 2000 with the boom in dot com companies. It is a real and profound opportunity for countries around the world to increase the pace and scope of the benefits of development. It marks a significant shift in the relative importance of different resources or factors of production in the development process.

Knowledge Revolution

- By one recent estimate, 50-60 per cent of all industrial output is based on information.
- Modern manufacturing industries depend as much for their success on the management of information relating to quality, cost and scheduling, as they do on the management of materials and production processes.
- The services sector, which has the great potential for creating new employment opportunities and economic growth in the world economy, is essentially knowledge-based.
- The phenomenal growth of employment potential in this century has been mostly driven by the rapid expansion of small and medium, technology intensive sectors and services.

This shift from material to knowledge-based resources opens up vast opportunities for the developing countries to accelerate the pace of development. India's rate of economic growth can be substantially increased if the country becomes a superpower in knowledge and if the potentials of information and information technology are fully understood and exploited.

Thus far, the potentials have been narrowly focused on the export potentials of the IT sector. But far greater potential lies in the extension and application of IT to stimulate the development of other sectors of the domestic economy. Information is a revolutionary force in bridging the digital divide that currently separates the advantaged and the disadvantaged of our nation. Apart from generating new employment opportunities, the application of IT can vastly extend access to education, health care, markets, financial services, vocational skills, administrative services and other aspects of modern society, to many more people at far lower cost. It can dramatically reduce the cost of communications, improve access to technology and marketing capabilities for the rural poor, eliminate intermediary exploitation in the production and distribution chains, increase government accountability and stimulate democratic participation. Therefore, rather than addressing IT as a specific sector, in this report, we have chosen to highlight its significant contributions under different headings, like employment, education, infrastructure and governance.

Knowledge Resources

There are a host of non-material, knowledge-based human resources that we possess in abundance and can apply to achieve far greater results.

Knowledge Resources

- Technology
- Organisation
- Information
- Education
- Skills

Technology: Knowledge in the form of information technology (IT) has opened up the opportunity for India to become the premier, low-cost provider of computer software and IT-enabled services to the industrialised world. It can not only provide high paying jobs and rising exports, but also transform the way we educate our youth — increasing the speed, quality and efficiency of learning manifold. In addition, it can and is already transforming the way we communicate among ourselves and with the rest of the world, shrinking the distances between hemispheres, providing instantaneous access to the whole world's knowledge base and customer base. Knowledge in the form of biotechnology offers not only a lucrative field for employment and economic growth, but a means for improving the health of our people and the productivity of our fields. In the form of agricultural technology, knowledge can increase crop yields from the present level, which is far below world averages, to levels two, three or four times higher. Pioneering Indian farmers have already achieved it for a variety of crops. What they have done individually, we can do as a nation. Finally, knowledge in the form of manufacturing technology will raise the competitiveness of the Indian manufactures to international standards of costs and quality.

Organisation: Technology is not the only knowledge resource now abundantly at our disposal. Today we have access to the whole world's experience in organisation. Organisation is nothing but the know-how for carrying out work most efficiently and expeditiously. India's highly successful Green Revolution and White Revolution were the results of organisational innovations as much as technology. We have the opportunity to fashion new and better forms of organisation to carry out the tasks of education, health-delivery, governance, commerce, industry and social welfare.

Information: Physical and biological reactions require the presence of catalytic agents to set them in motion and speed completion. Human social processes depend on a catalytic agent too and that catalyst is information. Free movement of information releases society from fear of uncertainties. Information about prices and market potentials spurs an entrepreneur into commercial activity. Information about scientific and technological discovery prompts a scientist or an engineer to adopt new innovations and practical applications. Widely disseminated public information about proper health care and nutrition contributes more powerfully to the general health of the community than does a hospital or medical innovation. Information about government policies enables individuals and communities to fully exercise their rights and take advantage of public programmes. Information about distant places spurs tourism and trade. Information in all forms and all fields — administration, commerce, education, finance, health, science and technology — is the very source from which we shape our dreams, plans, decisions and actions. The more and better the quality of that information, the more enlightened, expansive, productive and effective will be our efforts at individual and social advancement.

Today, the average Indian citizen has access to a wider range of timely and reliable information than had the government leaders in the world's most advanced nations a few decades ago. The fairly easy access to computers and the Internet has placed the world at our fingertips. Spread of information is further facilitated by the advancement of telecommunications technology, rapid expansion of cellular telephone networks, as well as the recent legalisation of Internet telephony, that makes live voice communication possible at a fraction of the cost, both within the country and internationally.

Education: What is true of information is true of education as well. Dissemination of useful information can be said to constitute the so-called unorganised sector of public education. The formal educational system is its organised counterpart. Education is the process whereby society passes on the accumulated knowledge and experience of past generations to its youth in a systematic and abridged form, so that the next generation can start off where past generations have ended and move on from there. Today, through education we have access not only to the knowledge of our own direct ancestors but to the accumulated experience and wisdom of people the world over. With the development of modern media that brings sound and video images into every household, and with the advent of the Internet that enables us to reach out to sources of knowledge around the world, education offers both unprecedented richness of content and the capacity to deliver it. If only we could break free from the limitations of out-dated curriculum and out-moded delivery systems, we could utilise the opportunity to close the education gap that separates the world's most prosperous communities from their poorer cousins.

Skills: Productive skills form another component of the precious human resource that we can and must fully utilise as leverage for national development. Skill is the ability to direct human energy efficiently to achieve desirable goals. A large reserve of unskilled people may be perceived as a problem, but a large population of skilled workers is a huge asset. It takes both knowledge and skill to train people and we have these in abundance. Imparting employable skills to our entire workforce is not only highly desirable but highly achievable as well.

All the resources that we have enumerated — technology, organisation, information, education and skill — are knowledge-based resources. Knowledge-based resources differ significantly in character from material resources. While material resources are consumed when they are utilised, knowledge resources increase when shared. Material resources are costly to transport and store, whereas knowledge resources are easily transportable at rapid speed and can be stored at negligible cost.

Historically, development has occurred under conditions in which access to critical resources was restricted to a relatively small portion of the population. The distinct characteristic of knowledge as a resource makes it possible, for the first time, to spread and share a resource among the entire population. The pace of India's future progress will depend to a large extent on its ability to make available the latest and most useful knowledge to vast sections of the population.

3

Human Development

The People

Human beings are distinguished among all living species by their capacity to develop and think. Though development is often measured in terms of so many miles of roads, number of tall buildings, airports, cars, TVs, computers etc., it is not things and places alone that define development. Development must be people centric. Twenty years hence, the people of India will be more numerous, better educated, healthier and more prosperous than at any other time in our long history. Having eradicated the scourge of famine that plagued the country for centuries, we still confront the challenging tasks of providing a nutritious diet to all our children, educating our teeming masses, abolishing epidemic diseases and creating employment opportunities for all our citizens.

Today India is the second most populous country in the world, with about 1.04 billion people, home to a-sixth of humanity. Although it is difficult to accurately predict population growth rates 20 years to the future, we expect this number to rise by another 300-350 million, in spite of continuous efforts to reduce fertility rates. This would raise the total population to about 1330 million by 2020.

India is in the process of a demographic transition from high fertility, high mortality and stable population to low fertility, low mortality and stable population. This transition is a global phenomenon generated by the improved availability and access to modern health care that sharply reduced mortality rates and increased life expectancy. The Crude death rate has declined to one-third of its level in 1941 and the expectation of life at birth has nearly doubled during this period. Falling mortality rates have been followed by a steady decline in birth rates, but this decline has not been as steep as the fall in death rate; even after reaching the replacement fertility rates, the population will continue to grow because of large numbers of young persons entering reproductive age.

While assessing future prospects, it is necessary to take into account the vast regional differences in demographic parameters. Population growth has recently decelerated below 2 per cent for the first time in four decades, but not uniformly across the length and breadth of the country. Several states in south India have already reached, or are about to attain, the replacement level of fertility that would ensure a zero growth rate of population in the long run. On the other hand, in many states in north India, characterised by high fertility rates, it may take several decades to reach the replacement level of fertility. There are also similar differentials in levels of mortality, especially in infant and child mortality.

At the national level, two alternate scenarios for achieving population stabilisation have been considered. In the optimistic scenario, which is based on achieving the demographic goals of the National Population Policy 2000, life expectancy is assumed to rise to 71 for males and 74 for females by 2020. Under the realistic scenario, life expectancy is assumed to reach 65 for males and 69 for females by 2020. Under either scenario India's population would exceed 1.3 billion in the year 2020.

In both cases the sex ratio of population (females per 1000 males) would marginally increase from 932 in 2000 to 950 in 2020; reversing the historical trend of falling sex ratio is expected in the 21st Century.

We can be more certain of the changes in the age structure of the population as given in Table 2.

Actually, the population under-15 years is expected to increase only marginally over the next 20 years. This means that pressure for expansion of the educational system will come only from increasing enrolment and efforts to reduce drop-out rates.

Table – 2

Population Projections (millions)

Year	2000	2005	2010	2015	2020
Total	1010	1093	1175	1256	1331
Under 15	361	368	370	372	373
15-64	604	673	747	819	882
65+	45	51	58	65	76

Source: Based on P.N. Mari Bhatt, "Indian Demographic Scenario 2025", Institute of Economic Growth, New Delhi, Discussion Paper No. 27/2001.

The largest growth of population will be in the 15-64 year age group, which will expand by about 46 per cent by 2020 (i.e., annually by 1.9 per cent as against the population growth of much lower, at 1.4 per cent). As shown in Table 2, it is expected to rise from 604 million in 2000 to 883 million in 2020, i.e., from 60 to 66 per cent of the total population. This rise will accentuate the need for challenge of reducing fertility and increasing employment opportunities, so that the family size comes down and incomes rise.

The elderly population is also expected to rise sharply from 45 to 76 million, (i.e., by 2.6 per cent per annum) and their share in the total population would rise from 4.5 to 5.7 per cent. As a consequence of these age structural changes, the age-dependency ratio (ratio of non-working age population to working age population) is expected to fall from 67 per cent in 2000 to 46 per cent in 2020, although the percentage of elderly people to population will increase.

Food Security

The single most important implication of India's rapid population growth during the second half of the twentieth century was the threat it posed to national food security. That threat reached dangerous proportions in the mid-1960s, leading to the launching of the Green Revolution, achievement of food self-sufficiency, and subsequently, a growing stock of surplus food grains by the mid-1970s. Happily, such a threat no longer exists for the country. Growth of food production has exceeded population growth for each of the past three decades.

Statistics present a confusing picture of India's progress on food security. Both per capita food grain consumption and total calorific intake have declined slightly in recent years among all levels of the population. At the same time, grain surpluses have reached peak levels and real per capita expenditure on food is rising among all income groups. The factors influencing this trend are numerous and complex, however, it can be primarily attributed to:

- Reduction in calorie requirement due to a more sedentary life style among both the rural and urban population. Bicycle and bus travel, mechanised pumps and equipments, access to telephones and newspapers have reduced the physical work to a greater or lesser extent for most Indians.
- Diversification of the Indian diet to include a larger intake of fruits, vegetables, dairy products, sugar, oil and pulses, eggs, fish and meat products, thereby reducing the required intake of calories from cereals.

However, the challenge of achieving food security for all our people remains a real one even today, and will continue to demand our attention in the coming decades. Food security depends on both availability of food and access to it. Long-term food security requires not only producing sufficient food to meet the market demand, but also ensuring that all citizens have the required purchasing power to obtain the food they need for a nutritious and healthy life. India has won the first battle, but the second still looms large. By best estimates, nearly half of the population still suffers from chronic under-nutrition. The most vulnerable are children, women and the elderly, specially among the lower income groups. While the number of children suffering from severe malnutrition declined significantly in the 1990s, the prevalence of mild and moderate under-nutrition, especially among those in the lower 30 per cent income group, is still high. Prevalence of micro nutrient deficiencies such as anaemia is also very high.

The problem of chronic macro and micro nutrient under-nutrition cannot be addressed simply by increases in food production or the accumulation of larger food buffer stocks. Nor has the public distribution system been able to effectively target the most needy in an effective manner. Targeted food for work programmes and targeted nutrition programmes can alleviate the problem temporarily. But in the long run, the solution is to ensure employment opportunities for all citizens so that they acquire the purchasing power to meet their nutritional requirements. Thus, employment or livelihood security becomes an essential and inseparable component of a comprehensive strategy for national food security and must be considered as one of the nation's highest priorities.

Increasing food consumption alone is not a sufficient condition for overcoming malnutrition in India. It is also necessary to address the factors responsible for the high incidence of gastrointestinal and respiratory infections as well as cultural factors responsible for faulty child feeding and weaning practices. Assured provision of safe drinking water, improved health care and education for all women are necessary elements of a comprehensive strategy to eliminate malnutrition and achieve the goal of Food for All before 2020.

India's population is still rapidly expanding. Living standards are rising and slated to rise faster than in the past. As they rise, both calorific intake and diversification of diet will increase significantly. Although a portion of this increase can and will be obtained from abroad, a fulfilling vision of India 2020 depicts this nation — with its conducive and varied climate, the largest irrigated area in the world and a vast farming population — as a major food exporter. Both as a challenge and as an opportunity, India can and must do much more to modernise and diversify its agriculture to meet the increased domestic and international demand for a wide variety of food products.

Continued growth of the agriculture sector is particularly important because it plays such a vital role in generating purchasing power among the rural population. Therefore, it is essential that agricultural development strategies for the 21st Century focus on generating both higher incomes and greater on-farm and off-farm employment opportunities.

India is now entering the fourth stage of agricultural transformation. The Green Revolution phase spread in the north-western and southern states from the mid-1960s to the mid-1980s. From the early 1980s, it spread rapidly in the central, and to a lesser extent the eastern states. This, coupled with a further growth of productivity in the north-western and southern states, enabled India to achieve a 3.77 per cent annual growth rate in agricultural production during the 1980s. The overall growth slowed to 2.72 per cent in the 1990s, which was associated with a reduction in public investment in both agriculture and agricultural research, slower growth of fertilizer consumption and the area under high yielding varieties, and degradation of soils.

Stages of Agricultural Development

1. Pre-Green Revolution	Boost in productivity growth of coarse grains and pulses per unit of land.
2. Green Revolution	Expansion of area and rapid growth in productivity of wheat and rice, made possible by widespread adoption of improved varieties, expansion of agricultural research, demonstration and education, and investment in irrigation, supported by establishment of a national infrastructure to produce and supply inputs and to warehouse, distribute and market outputs.
3. Post-Green Revolution	Continued growth in productivity through intensification of chemical and labour inputs, followed by a gradual deceleration in productivity growth. Expansion of area under maize, cotton, sugarcane, and oilseeds.
4. Commercialisation	Further diversification of cropping patterns from low value to high value crops such as fruits, vegetables, flowers and other horticulture crops for domestic consumption, processing and export.

There is enormous scope for accelerating growth in agriculture, through improved soil nutrition and pest management, diversification into higher value-added crops, expansion and more efficient use of irrigation potential, rainwater harvesting, and infrastructure development for agro-processing industries. India's productivity on major crops ranks far below the world average. This low productivity contributes to low farm incomes and wages, lower on-farm employment generation, and relatively high food prices for all Indians. Average yields from tomato cultivation, for example, are 76 per cent higher in Mexico and more than four times higher in the USA, while average yields on seed cotton are more than four times higher in Mexico and three times higher in USA. Even within India, some progressive farmers have achieved yields comparable to their foreign counterparts till recently; but these high achievers are a rare exception. Progressive farming must become the rule and the standard. Raising the productivity of our soil and water resources is an effective way to increase the profit margins of farmers, while at the same time reducing the cost of farm produce, so that it is more affordable to the masses. A minimum target should be to double or triple the average yields of major commercial crops. This will reduce pressure on scarce land and water resources as well as enable the country to utilise less fertile areas for other purposes.

Tapping the full potential of Indian agriculture to meet the rising domestic demand and to take advantage of the liberalisation of international trade will require, first and foremost, the recognition of the vital role that agriculture can continue to play in national development. The other necessary conditions are: greater public investment in research; expansion and development of rural infrastructure including roads, storage capacity and organised markets; improved farmer education; effective involvement of the private sector to provide technology, investment and organisational expertise for commercialisation; and modification of land regulations to achieve greater production efficiency. A suitable land use pattern will also need to be implemented, based on the principle that each region would focus on crops best suited to their agro-climatic characteristics, soil types and water resources. Strong measures will also be needed to address the problem of land degradation that affects an estimated 45 per cent of total land area. India's objective for 2020 must not only be to produce the food its population requires but also to fully exploit the comparative advantages it possesses — agro-climatic variety, irrigation, scientific capabilities and low labour cost — to become a low cost, high profit producer for the world market.

Figure 1 depicts the projected food production under two scenarios, together with estimates of food demand in 2020. Business-as-usual (BAU) assumes that growth of production continues at the same rates as during the 1990s. The Best-case scenario (BCS) assumes that production grows at the higher rates achieved during the 1980s. Even under the BAU, India will be able to meet the projected demand in all five food categories. This indicates that more emphasis can be placed on diversifying production to other value added agricultural products.

Figure 1

Current & Projected Food Production vs. Demand in 2020

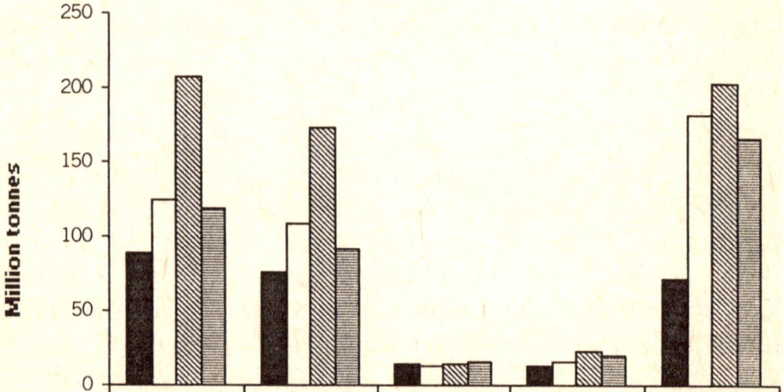

	Rice	Wheat	Coarse Cereals	Pulses	Milk
■ 2000	89	76	13.6	13.5	71
□ 2020 BAU	125	108	13	16	181
▧ 2020 BCS	207	173	14	23	203
▤ 2020 Demand	119	92	15.6	19.5	166

Source: Based on R. Radhakrishnan and K. Venkata Reddy, "Vision 2020: Food Security and Nutrition", paper prepared for Planning Commission.

India needs to sustain an agricultural growth rate of 4.0 to 4.5 per cent in order to reduce food insecurity and poverty, while increasing rural purchasing power. At this growth rate, agricultural development could more rapidly diversify into horticulture, fishery, dairying, animal husbandry and other areas. It would also spur the growth of agro-processing industries in rural areas. Such an achievement is well within reach, provided there is the requisite commitment to raising crop productivity through dissemination of advanced technologies; increasing investment in irrigation, research and training; water harvesting and improved access to credit.

While food production should be able to comfortably meet the total domestic demand, there will still be sections of the population that require assistance in order to meet their nutritional requirements. In view of the high cost and inefficiency of the public food distribution system, reform should directly target the most vulnerable sections, which can be more effectively accomplished through programmes such as food vouchers or food stamps. For the vast majority of the population, food security can best be achieved by ensuring creation of gainful employment opportunities for all job seekers.

Employment

Population, food security, education and remunerative employment opportunities are closely interconnected. Rising levels of education and rising living standards are powerful levers for reducing birth and mortality rates. As population growth slows to replacement levels over the next two decades, India's greatest challenge will be to expand the opportunities for the growing labour force, to enrich their knowledge and skills through education, raise their living standards through gainful employment and make provisions for ensuring a good life for the aged. India has met the challenge of producing sufficient food to feed everyone, but it has yet to meet the challenge of generating sufficient employment opportunities to ensure that all its people have the purchasing power to obtain the food they require. Gainful employment is one of the most essential conditions for food security and economic security. Conversely, food security is an essential requirement for raising the productivity of India's workforce to international levels.

India's labour force has reached 375 million approximately in 2002, and it will continue to expand over the next two decades. The actual rate of that expansion will depend on several factors including population growth, growth of the working age population, labour force participation rates, educational enrolment at higher levels and school drop-out rates. Projections based on these parameters indicate that India's labour force will expand by 7 to 8.5 million per year during the first decade of this century, and will increase by a total of about 160-170 million by 2020, i.e., 2.0 per cent per annum.

Total unemployment in India has been estimated to be about 35 million persons in 2002. This figure takes into account the significant level of underemployment and seasonal variations in the availability of work. It also reflects wide variations in the rate of unemployment among different age groups and regions of the country. Approximately three-fourth of the unemployed are in rural areas and three-fifth among them are educated. The recent trends towards shedding excess labour to improve competitiveness and increasing capital intensity have further aggravated the situation. A clear consensus is now emerging that major changes in economic policy and strategy will be needed to meet the country's employment needs.

Future rates of unemployment will depend on a range of factors, including the growth rate of the labour force and changes in the structure of employment between different sectors, as well as the growth rate of the economy. Adopting the higher number takes us closer to understanding the full magnitude of the challenge the country faces for providing employment opportunities for all its people. India needs to generate on the order of 200 million additional employment opportunities over the next 20 years.

The first question that inevitably arises is whether generating nine or ten million jobs a year is feasible, and that naturally begets the question of what rates of economic growth would be required for achieving this. However logical and inevitable it may sound, we believe this is the wrong way to approach the problem. The right question to ask is: How important is it to us as a nation to create employment opportunities for all? The answer here is simple. It is extremely important. It is as important to create job opportunities for all citizens in a market economy as it is to provide universal suffrage to all adults in a democracy. Access to employment is an essential component of freedom of economic choice. Absence of such opportunity means depriving our young not only of economic freedom but of hope as well. India's vision for 2020 must be founded on the premise of gainful Jobs for All. Access to employment should not only be a top priority of the government but a constitutionally guaranteed fundamental human right.

But can we possibly achieve such an ambitious goal and that too within the framework of a non-subsidised market economy? In order to answer this question, first of all we need to recognise that the economy we build over the next two decades and the jobs we create will be products of the decisions we make, not some irreversible logic of economic science. It is we, the nation, that have to decide what we want to accomplish and how serious we are about doing it, how willing we are to change our attitudes and to alter our policies to achieve this desirable goal. We conclude that if the will and determination are present, the goal is achievable.

Achieving full employment will require a reorientation of national priorities, technology policy and government action. Until now, planning to achieve national goals has been largely done on a sector-wise basis by respective ministries assigned with the responsibility. These parallel lines of planning need to be integrated around a central vision and set of goals, of which full employment must be one. As we have incorporated an environmental analysis into all our planning, every plan initiative needs also to be re-evaluated to consider its impact on employment.

Despite a persistent tendency to associate employment with large industry in the organised sector, an in-depth examination of employment potentials makes it evident that the largest share of new jobs will come from the unorganised sector. In evaluating the importance of developing each sector, we must include an assessment of its potential contribution to employment. Such an assessment will have to be made for the unorganised sector, which currently contributes 92 per cent of the country's employment and generates seven times greater labour intensity per unit of production, as compared to the organised sector. The public organised sector has been and will continue to shed jobs. Although the private organised sector will contribute significantly to the growth of the economy, its contribution to the overall employment generation will be quite modest, since total employment in this sector currently represents only 2.5 per cent of all jobs. Even if this sector grows by 30 per cent per annum, over five years it will contribute less than one per cent to the growth of the workforce.

International comparisons reveal that small and medium enterprises (SMEs) create the majority of jobs. In the USA, nearly half of the private workforce is employed in small firms, of which three-fifth have less than five employees. In Japan, 78 per cent of jobs are generated by small and medium enterprises. The small and medium manufacturing enterprises in Korea account for 99 per cent of all manufacturing enterprises and 69 per cent of employment in this sector. Therefore, the unorganised sector, including small and medium enterprises, must play a central role in the country's employment strategy. This will require modification of policies and programmes to level the playing field, improve availability of credit, increase productivity, raise quality consciousness and competitiveness, and enhance job quality.

Recent experiences of different countries in the context of globalisation also demonstrate that SMEs are better insulated from the pressures generated by the volatility of world trade and capital markets. They are more resistant to the stresses, and more responsive to the demands of the fast-changing technologies and entrepreneurial responses. Indeed, they are observed to be a very important vehicle for new technology adoption and entrepreneurial development. What is true of the most developed countries today will be true for India in 2020. SMEs will play a crucial role in ensuring India's international competitiveness and its rapid assimilation of new technologies.

An assessment of the different sectors reveals a vast untapped employment potential in a wide range of fields for unskilled, semi-skilled, skilled and professionally educated workers. Table 3 provides a list of specific sectors with the largest gross employment potential per unit of output.

The growth of food grain production may not lead to a significant growth in on-farm employment opportunities. However, there is substantial scope for creating new jobs through watershed development programmes, expansion of the area under irrigated cultivation, raising crop yields which increases labour intensity, and diversification of cropping patterns into cash crops — especially vegetables and horticultural crops. Together, these could generate upwards of 20 to 30 million new on-farm employment opportunities during the next decade.

Table – 3

High Employment Potential Sectors

- Commercial agriculture
- Agro-industry & agri-business
- Afforestation for pulp, fuel & power
- Retail and wholesale trade
- Tourism
- Housing
- Construction
- Garment industry
- Other small scale & medium industries
- IT & IT enabled services
- Education
- Health
- Financial services
- Transport
- Communications
- Community services

Source: Compiled from Planning Commission documents.

India processes less than 2 per cent of its fruit and vegetable products, as compared with 70 to 80 per cent in countries such as Brazil, Malaysia and Philippines. The development of downstream processing, packaging and distribution activities can generate millions of additional off-farm jobs. Policies are needed to attract greater private sector participation in terms of land development, production and processing technologies, investment, management and marketing. A concerted effort to fully develop the potentials of agri-business could generate millions of additional jobs.

The recorded forest area constitutes about 23 per cent of the geographical area (about 71 million hectares) of the country, but half of this area is degraded. Hence, it is unable to play an important role in environmental sustainability and in meeting the forest produce needs of the people, the industry and other sectors. India has more than 50 million hectares of degraded wasteland that lie outside the national forests, in addition to 30 million hectares within protected areas. In spite of this huge expanse, the country is a net importer of forest products to the extent of $2.5 billion annually. Afforestation of India's vast expanse of wastelands and depleted forest areas for production of wood pulp, timber, fuel, fodder, biomass power, edible and fuel soil, fuel, herbs and medicinal plants for exports can create millions of jobs, while reversing environmental degradation and supporting industrial development. Every two hectares of additional area placed under plantation of forest crop such as bamboo, casuarina, eucalyptus or oil-bearing plants can generate year-round employment for one person. Development of forests can generate 10 to 15 million additional employment opportunities over the next five year plan period and increase the livelihood opportunities of low income families during the transition period, while educational levels are rising and other sectors of the economy are developing.

The contribution of primary sector employment to the total workforce has been coming down very slowly, to 56-57 per cent in 1999-2000, and should decrease to about 51 per cent by 2006-2007. This slow rate of decline is likely to continue for at least a decade, because of the hidden under-employment in the agriculture sector, partly compensated for by the vast potential for additional job creation by crop diversification and afforestation. Increasing prosperity in agriculture will naturally lead to the growth of non-farm jobs in agri-industries, agro-business and other occupations required to meet the needs of an increasingly prosperous farming community. During the second decade of the 21st Century, increasing domestic demand for manufactured products and services, coupled with more rapid mechanisation of agriculture will draw in more and more people to non-farm occupations. By 2020, total employment in agriculture may fall to less than 45 per cent, while the share of the services sector increases proportionately.

The small scale industries (SSI) sector accounts for 95 per cent of industrial units, 40 per cent of value addition, 35 per cent of exports, and 80 per cent of manufacturing employment. Registered SSI units provide nearly 18 million jobs in the country at this time. Among manufacturing sectors, the single largest employment potential is in textiles, which is slated to generate 7 million jobs over the next five years alone. More than 40 per cent of these jobs are in garment production units in the SSI sector. A healthy and rapidly expanding small sector is essential for a vibrant growth of the Indian economy as a whole. This sector serves as the field for entrepreneurship to flourish, as an entry point for new entrepreneurs who can start small and then grow, as a vehicle for extending the regional spread of industry, as a laboratory for development of innovative products and services, and as an essential support to attract large manufacturing assembling industries from overseas. Since SSIs are generally more employment intensive per unit of capital than large scale industry, they are also a source of much needed employment. Employment in the registered SSI sector has nearly tripled over the past 20 years. A repetition of this performance would generate an additional 36 million jobs over the next 20 years. A comprehensive package of venture capital, credit, liberalisation of controls, technical training, marketing and management measures is needed to ensure the continuous expansion of this sector.

By far, the largest number of new jobs will be in the services sector. Over the past 100 years, the US economy has more than quadrupled the total number of those employed, yet the percentage of the US workforce engaged in manufacturing is now back to the same level as it was in 1850, while agricultural employment has shrunk to less than 3 per cent of the US workforce. Today, the fastest growing job categories in the USA are in services industries such as financial services, insurance, education, health, construction and real estate. Rapid growth is slated for a wide range of services in India, including professional, computer-related research and development, real estate, leasing, advertising, printing and packaging, marketing, telecommunications, postal and courier, audiovisual, engineering and construction, wholesale and retail distribution, all levels and types of education, environment, banking, insurance, health, travel, sports and recreation, and all categories of transport services. By the year 2020 more than 120 million jobs will come from the services sector alone.

Tourism-related occupations, including hotels and restaurants, employ 10.8 per cent of workers globally, compared to only 5.6 per cent in India. Domestic tourism will rise rapidly as living standards increase. India's domestic tourist sector is the fastest growing in the world, but with the lowest level of investment. The potential for international tourism too has not yet been exploited properly. China currently attracts more than five times as many foreign tourists, excluding visitors from Hong Kong. Thailand, Malaysia, and Turkey attract three to four times as many. By one estimate, development of India's tourism infrastructure such as roads, airports and medium priced hotels, combined with modifications in air and hotel pricing and tax policies, could generate more than 20 million additional employment opportunities in tourist related businesses within a decade.

Numerous studies have been undertaken to assess the potentials of the IT industry and to identify specific strategies needed to accelerate development of this sector. The NASSCOM-McKinsey study in 1999 projected creation of a $ 70 billion IT industry, employing more than two million persons within 10 years. The worldwide market for IT services is expected to exceed $900 billion by 2010.

The recent growth of IT-enabled service businesses in India — call centres, medical transcription, technical support and back office processing, engineering and design, geographic information services, payroll and other human resource services, insurance claim processing, legal databases — is powerful evidence that the potential of IT technology and knowledge based industries extends far beyond the development of software and hardware. The US experience shows that, as the application of information technology spreads and encompasses traditional industries, it can generate new employment opportunities ten times greater in number than those directly involved in core IT industries.

IT is also a stimulant to the growth of home-based employment opportunities, especially suitable for women. The trend towards tele-working, which is growing rapidly in USA and some other countries, is just beginning in India. The lower cost and greater convenience of home-based employment is bound to open up greater job opportunities for educated women with children.

IT services will be a powerful engine of job growth, but the term 'Knowledge-based industries' includes a much wider range of commercial opportunities. It encompasses all fields in which the application of mind, judgment and skill, rather than the application of mechanised production technology is the core resource. Education, health services, biotechnology, pharmaceuticals, insurance and financial services are among the leading industries in this category. They are also among the fastest growing industries in the world. Added to these, there is enormous scope for other knowledge intensive activities such as clinical drug trials and many other types of scientific research.

The management of all types of information is emerging as a major growth industry worldwide and India is well poised to become a global leader in this field. Increasing demand for education within the country and worldwide will create tremendous demand for qualified teachers with adequate language skills. An estimated two million additional teachers will be needed in India to support 100 per cent primary school enrolment and to reduce the teacher-student ratio for improved quality of teaching. Another two million or more will be required to support higher rates of upper primary and secondary school education and to reduce teacher-student ratios at those levels. Teaching staff for vocational training and higher education need to be expanded as well.

Demand for health services is increasing worldwide. Already nurses and medical technicians are in short supply. The USA has a doctor-nurse ratio of about twice that of India. Yet the US currently faces a shortfall of nurses, that is more than three times India's total annual production of new nurses. Physicians, nurses, medical technicians and other scientific occupations will become growth industries to rival the IT sector within the next decade. Creation of new jobs in existing industries can and should be supplemented by creation of new services industries that will in turn stimulate increased employment opportunities.

It is extremely difficult to project unemployment rates 20 years into the future, when so much doubt exists even about current levels of unemployment and underemployment. However, it is clear that rising levels of education and growth of the 60 plus age group will mitigate to some extent the growth of the labour force. Combined with the enormous opportunities for creation of new employment opportunities, the incidence of unemployment should be almost eliminated during the second decade of the century.

Education

Successful population policy is directly linked to successful education policy. Success in raising literacy rates and school enrolment rates while reducing drop-out rates, especially for women, are closely correlated with the delayed onset of marriage and child birth, improved mortality for both mothers and children, and reduction in family size. In fact, a successful education policy forms the bedrock of all fields of national development — political, economic, technical, scientific, social, and environmental. Education is the foundation for a vibrant democracy in which informed citizens exercise their franchise to support the internal growth of the nation and its constructive role in the world community. It is the foundation for growth in productivity, incomes and employment opportunities and for the development, application and adaptation of science and technology to enhance the quality of life. Education is the foundation for access to the benefits of the information revolution that is opening up vistas on the whole world. Education is also the foundation for improved health care and nutrition.

Literacy, the basis of all education, is as essential to survival and development in modern society as food is to survival and development of the human body. Literacy rates in India have arisen dramatically from 18 per cent in 1951 to 65 per cent in 2001, but these rates are still far from the UMI reference level of 95 per cent. Literacy must be considered the minimum right and requirement of every Indian citizen. Vast differences also remain among different sections of the population. Literacy among males is nearly 50 per cent higher than females, and it is about 50 per cent higher in urban areas as compared to the rural areas. Literacy rates range from as high as 96 per cent in some districts of Kerala to below 30 per cent in some parts of Madhya Pradesh. Rates are also significantly lower among scheduled castes and tribes than among other communities.

These differential rates of progress leave approximately 300 million illiterate adults in the country, the largest number of illiterates in the world. For these people, the traditional avenues of knowledge dissemination through education and printed information are ruled out. These are the people who are most vulnerable to the challenges of development, because they are least equipped to rapidly expand their knowledge base. Since many of them are relatively young adults who will still be active in 2020, the country cannot afford to ignore them or leave them behind. The Government has already set a goal to achieve 75 per cent literacy by the end of the Tenth Five Year Plan. A 100 per cent literate India is of paramount importance for realising the vision for the country in 2020 as presented in this document. Even when this goal is achieved, innovative approaches will be needed to increase knowledge dissemination through TV and other means, to literate adults with little or no formal education.

Literacy is an indispensable minimum condition for development, but it is not sufficient. In this increasingly complex and technologically sophisticated world, ten years of school education must also be considered as an essential prerequisite for citizens to adapt and succeed economically, avail of the social opportunities and develop their individual potentials. Education is the primary and most effective means so far evolved for transmitting practically useful knowledge from one generation to another.

India's education system has expanded exponentially over the past five decades, but its current achievements are grossly inadequate for the nation to realise its potential greatness. The net enrolment rate in primary schools is around 77 per cent and in secondary schools it is around 60 per cent. These compare with the 99.9 per cent primary and 69 per cent secondary enrolment for the UMI reference level. The drop out rate was 40 per cent at the primary level and 55 per cent at the upper primary level in 1999-2000. These high drop out rates from both primary and secondary school, combined with low enrolment rates at the higher levels deprive tens of millions of children of their full rights as citizens. Out of approximately 200 million children in the age group 6-14 years, only 120 million are in schools and net attendance in the primary level is only 66 per cent of the enrolment. Further, less than 7 per cent of the children ever pass the 10th standard public examination.

Apart from addressing the needs of a large illiterate population, India's knowledge strategy must also develop innovative approaches to enhance knowledge acquisition among the large community of school drop-outs. Unless something is done to drastically reduce drop-out rates, by the year 2016 there will be approximately 500 million people in the country with less than five years of schooling, and another 300 million that will not have completed high school. In other words, about two-thirds of the population will lack the minimum level of education needed to keep pace with and take advantage of the social changes occurring within the country and worldwide.

Extending the primary school system to over 500,000 villages in India has brought education to the masses. Unfortunately, this huge quantitative expansion has been accompanied by a tremendous dilution in the quality of schooling. High drop out rates in rural areas is one result of single room schools, with few teaching aids and inadequate instruction both in terms of quantity and quality. Qualitative improvement in the system can be accomplished by promoting centralised schools serving clusters of 10 or more villages, wherever distances and transportation links make that feasible. This will permit greater investment in educational infrastructure, including introduction of computers.

Achieving 100 per cent enrolment of all children in the 6 to 14 year age group is an ambitious but achievable goal for 2020. This must be coupled with efforts to increase the quality and relevance of school curriculum to equip students not only with academic knowledge but also with the values and practical knowledge needed for success in life. Table 4 depicts a business-as usual scenario for primary and secondary education in 2020, based on recent trends as well as an alternative scenario designed to radically enhance the quantity and quality of school education in the country.

A tremendous expansion of schools and classrooms will be required to support a quantitative and qualitative improvement in the country's school system. In order to achieve the best-case scenario depicted in Table 4, total school enrolment would have to increase by 75 million or 44 per cent. That will require a proportionate expansion in the number of classrooms. In addition, efforts to improve the quality of education by reducing the class size would require a further 20 per cent increase in the number of classrooms. Together, this will necessitate increasing the total number of classrooms by 65 per cent within 20 years.

Table – 4

Education Scenarios in 2020

	1980 Actual	2000 Estimated	2020 Business-as-usual	2020 Best-case Scenario
Primary enrolment (1-5)	80%	89%	100%	100%
Elementary enrolment (1-8)	77%	79%	85%	100%
Secondary enrolment (9-12)	30%	58%	75%	100%
Drop-out rate (1-5)	54%	40%	20%	0%
Drop-out rate (1-8)	73%	54%	35%	0%

Source: Garry Jacobs "Vision 2020: Towards a Knowledge Society", paper prepared for Planning Commission.

An enormous increase in the number of teachers will also be required to achieve the alternative scenario, i.e., eliminating primary school drop outs and reducing the teacher-pupil ratio from the present high level of 1:42 down to around 1:20, which is the UMI reference level. Together, this will require an additional three million primary school teachers, more than twice the number currently employed. Similar increases will be required at middle and secondary school levels. The training of such large number of teachers will require the establishment of additional teacher training colleges and much larger budget allocations for teachers' salaries.

Qualitative improvements in education should reflect a change in pedagogical methods and lay emphasis on several dimensions, including:

- A shift from methods that emphasize passive learning to those that foster the active interest and ability of children to learn on their own.
- A shift from rote memorisation to development of children's capacity for critical thinking.
- A shift from traditional academic to practically relevant curriculum.
- A shift from imparting information to imparting life values such as independent thinking, self-reliance and individual initiative that are essential for success in any field of endeavour.

An important role of education is to foster in each child the attributes and values of a responsible, capable, active and healthy member of the family and society. The rigidity of curriculum, testing and teaching methods need to be relaxed so that innovative methods and new models of education can be evolved, tested and perfected. Vocational streams have to be developed and expanded to equip larger numbers of high school students with occupation-related knowledge and skills.

Experimentation is needed with new methods for knowledge delivery. Television can be a very effective means for educating both school going and non-school going children and adults. It can deliver teaching materials in a more dynamic, entertaining, and interesting manner, utilising the nation's best teachers and multimedia teaching materials on each subject. A TV based curriculum can help slow learners to supplement classroom teaching, fast learners to learn at much faster rates than the rest of the class, drop outs to acquire knowledge they missed out in school, and adults to expand their level of education without returing to school.

New methods of delivery will be particularly necessary to augment access and improve delivery at higher levels of education. Although India's college and university network has expanded dramatically as shown in Table 5, it is able to accommodate only a tiny fraction of the college-age population. In addition, the quality of facilities, teaching and course materials leaves much to be desired. Recruitment and promotion are highly politicised; seniority rule precludes merit advancement; and the cost of delivery is beyond the means of the vast majority of young Indians.

Table – 5

Growth of Higher Educational Institutions

Years	Colleges for General Education	Colleges for Professional Education	Universities
1951	370	208	27
1998	7199	2075	229

Source: Department of Education, Govt. of India.

India in 2020 must be a nation in which all those who aspire for higher education have access to college and university level courses. A national network of community colleges, similar to the highly successful American system, is needed to provide knowledge and job-oriented skills to millions of young people who lack interest in or capacity for more stringent academic studies.

The advent of computer and the Internet-based educational methods offer an exciting new learning medium that can literally transform our concept of school and classroom from physical into virtual realities. Studies in the USA project a radical reshaping of higher education over the next two decades as a result of the digital revolution. Many traditional colleges will close as more course works are delivered at a distance through alternative channels. The traditional boundaries between education and other sectors will fade, as publishers, for-profit and non-profit organisations, offer accredited, multimedia-enhanced courses directly to students, by-passing the university. The traditional classroom type of education, which is most useful for students that require personal attention and assistance and for subjects that involve hands-on experimentation, will no longer be the predominant model of education. For all other purposes, it is very costly and not very efficient in the way it uses the time of both teachers and students.

Experience shows that computer-based educational methods can lead to much faster rates and higher quality of learning, which is more inter-active and motivating for students at all levels of education from pre-school to post-graduation. It is extremely effective for enhancing reading and language skills and general knowledge among the very young and even for some sophisticated professional courses such as medicine and engineering.

Given the huge number of young students that will quest for all levels of higher education in the coming decades and the severe shortage of qualified instructors, and in the light of India's outstanding expertise in the IT industry, the country needs to embark on a massive programme to convert the entire higher educational curriculum into a multi-media, web-based format and to establish accreditation standards for recognition of the distance education so imparted.

Our vision of India in 2020 is predicated on the belief that human resources are the most important determinants of overall development. As India's IT revolution has been fuelled by the availability of a very large reservoir of well-trained engineers, its future development in many different spheres will depend on commensurate development of sufficient and surplus capabilities.

Full development of India's enormous human potential will require a shift in national priorities, to commit a greater portion of the country's financial resources to the education sector. India currently invests 3.2-4.4 per cent of GNP on education. This compares unfavourably with the UMI reference level of 4.9 per cent, especially with countries such as South Africa, which invests 7.9 per cent of GNP on education. A near doubling of investments in education is the soundest policy for quadrupling the country's GDP per capita.

S&T Capabilities

Literacy and general education form the base of the knowledge pyramid that is essential for rapid and sustained development in the 21st century. The continuous advancement of science and application of improved technology form the middle rung; and social ideals and spiritual values form the apex.

Technical education, both vocational and professional, constitutes the foundation for development of science and technology. India is rightly proud of the international standing of its IITs, but a handful of world class technical institutions is not sufficient. A large number of the country's approximately 500 engineering colleges need to be upgraded to quality standards nearer to those of the IITs, and given similar autonomy. Private sector initiative and investment, whether from Indian corporates or NRIs or reputed foreign universities, need to be fully encouraged. Close links need to be fostered between technical institutions and industry.

India's enormous manpower base of scientists and engineers is often coveted. President Kalam observed that India's human resource base is one of its greatest core competencies. This is true in absolute terms, but as a percentage of the total population, we are at 1/100th of the US levels and 1/50th of the Korean level. Even China's manpower base of scientists and engineers as a percentage of its population exceeds ours by more than three times.

Absolute numbers do count, but manpower alone is not sufficient to excel in the development and application of science and technology. In terms of total investment in R&D, India's expenditure is 1/60th of that of Korea, 1/250th of that of the USA, and 1/340th of that of Japan. More significantly, atomic energy, space and defence research account for 71 per cent of all central spending on science and technology, which means that relatively little is left for investment in agriculture, energy, telecommunications and other crucial sectors within the sphere of science and technology. R&D expenditure even in India's fast-growing IT sector has been averaging around 3 per cent of sales turnover (STO), which is much lower as compared to the 14-19 per cent expended by internationally reputed software firms.

These low figures reflect on our R&D performance. India's share of global scientific output in 1998 was only 1.58 per cent of the world's total. Out of 500,000 new patent applications filed globally each year, China accounts for 96,000 and Korea accounts for 72,000, while India accounts for only 8,000. Of greater concern has been the country's inability to capitalise on our huge pool of manpower and extensive network of scientific research organisations for transferring proven technologies from the lab to the land and to the factory. Despite possessing the world's largest cadre of agricultural scientists, we have not been able to extend the momentum of Green Revolution to other regions and crops and to update the scientific practices of our farmers to levels comparable with most other nations. Crop productivity remains far below and production costs far above world averages. A similar gap exists in the application of science and technology for food processing and many other industries. High technology exports account for only 6 per cent of total manufacturing exports for India, compared to over 20 per cent for the UMI reference level.

India has a number of premier universities for scientific and technical education which produce world class scientists and engineers, but the national research system rarely produces world class results. One reason is the missing link between scientists in universities and research institutes and practitioners in agriculture and industry. Another is that non-teaching research institutes lack the continuous inflow of young talented researchers required to challenge assumptions and infiltrate new ideas and approaches. Bureaucracy, tenure and lack of accountability minimise the pressure for practical application of scientific knowledge. Other countries have done a much better job of providing optimum incentives to their scientific community and creating close linkages between science and industry. The management of technology and the administration of government require different sets of skills and a different culture. Management of technology demands innovation, global competitiveness, and wide latitude for individual freedom characteristics that are difficult to foster under an administrative regime.

The objectives of many institutes and the mechanisms for achieving them need a radical reorientation to bring them in tune with the changing environment brought about by liberalisation of imports, technology tie-ups with foreign agencies and foreign direct investment in key sectors. If the national R&D bodies do not reorganise themselves to face globalisation and global competition, nor take into consideration the nature of the factor endowment of the country along with many existing indigenous technologies so far neglected, then they risk becoming irrelevant to the mainstream activities of industrial development. The nature of service offered by these institutions has to undergo a sea change. Grass-root consultancy and turnkey project consultancy, including project implementation and monitoring are increasingly in demand.

Another essential step is to improve the linkages between technology development and technology application by fostering close ties between basic research and business. In the USA, a large proportion of scientific research at the university level is financed by business, and most leading universities operate technology incubators designed to promote commercialisation of new products and processes. India's recent experiment with the Science and Technology Entrepreneur Parks (STEPs) has been successful in promoting application of technologies, new business start-ups, and employment. The STEPs in combination with technology incubators need to be rapidly multiplied around the country. Effective R&D management backed by suitable incentives for commercialisation are essential for bridging the gap between the lab and the land or factory.

R&D is not only essential for propelling growth in industrial fields. It can also become a growth industry on its own. Much of the work done by Indian software companies for overseas clients and parent companies rightly fall under the category of new product development. Vast potential exists for complementing India's strengths in IT with corresponding strengthening of fields such as biotechnology, pharmaceuticals, designer-made materials, and others.

India's investment in the biotechnology sector is expected to increase five-fold by the end of the current decade, from US $2 billion to $ 10 billion, largely as a result of growing collaboration between multinational corporations and indigenous research efforts. Huge opportunities also exist for R&D in the field of genomics, bioinformatics, DNA technologies, clinical studies and genetically modified crops. Rationalisation of procedure, backed by effective bio-safety regulations are needed to govern testing and approval of biotech products.

India has the potential of converting its strong R&D infrastructure into a global research, design and development platform.

Vocational Training

The knowledge and skill of our workforce will be a major determinant of India's future rate of economic growth as well as the type and number of jobs we create. The greater that knowledge and skill, the higher will be the productivity, the better the quality, and the lower the cost of the products and services we generate. Similarly, the better the quality and lower the cost, greater will be the comparative advantage and market potential. Currently only 5 per cent of the country's labour force in the 20-24 age category have undergone formal vocational training, compared with 28 per cent in Mexico, 60 to 80 per cent in most industrialised nations, and as much as 96 per cent in Korea. A strategy to achieve full employment must include as an important component, a strategy to ensure that all new entrants to the workforce are equipped with the knowledge and skill needed for high productivity and high quality.

India has over 4,200 industrial training institutes (ITI) imparting education and training in 43 engineering and 24 non-engineering trades. Of these, 1,654 are government run ITIs, while 2,620 are private. The total seating capacity in these ITIs is 6.28 lakh. Most of this training is conducted in classroom style in the form of one to two year diploma courses. In addition, about 1.65 lakh persons undergo apprenticeship vocational training every year in state-run enterprises. If a wider definition of applied courses is taken that includes agriculture, engineering and other professional subjects, the total number receiving job related training is about 17 lakh per annum, which still represents only 14 per cent of new entrants to the workforce.

The nature of vocational skills makes it impossible for vocational schools to fully address the nation's needs. The variety of skills needed by the workforce is far too great. The changes in technology and work processes are too rapid for training courses and their instructors to stay up-to-date. The cost of training is also relatively high as it often demands full time enrolment for a prolonged period. Some vocational fields do not lend themselves to classroom or laboratory study at all.

A comprehensive strategy is thus needed to enhance the nation's employable skills. It must begin by preparing a catalogue of the entire range of vocational skills needed to support the development of the country. The network of vocational training institutes and the range of vocational skills taught needs to be expanded substantially to impart those skills for which institutional training is most suitable. The private sector, which promoted the rapid proliferation of computer training institutes throughout the country, should be encouraged to recognise the commercial potential of vocational training in many other fields.

In addition, it is essential to fashion more effective and efficient mechanisms for disseminating useful knowledge and skills, especially through the TV media and through computerised vocational training. The importance of computer has been widely recognised as a means to improve efficiency in business, government and formal education, but its application in vocational training is not fully appreciated.

Use of Computers in Vocational Training

- Rates of learning on computer for both academic as well as vocational or skill-based subjects are four to ten times faster than they are in a classroom setting, and learning retention is likely to be much higher.
- Computers can provide multimedia, interactive, customised and individually-paced learning with instantaneous feedback and testing.
- It eliminates the need for producing and deputing a large number of highly skilled instructors. Course contents can be rapidly modified to reflect changing needs.
- For many types of vocational skills, computerised training also offers specific advantages over the live delivery of skills in a classroom.
- Training can be delivered wherever computers are available. A nationwide network of 50,000 computerised vocational centres, run as private self-employed businesses similar to the STD booths and Internet cafes, can deliver low-cost, high-quality training to 10 million workers every year — more than five times the total number covered by existing programmes.

Although 58 per cent of Indians are engaged in agriculture, vocational training for farmers is one of the weakest links in the Indian educational system. Agricultural universities cater to the nation's need for agricultural scientists and extension officers. An extensive network of more than 300 Krishi Vignan Kendras (KVK) offers short and medium term courses for farmers on specialised subjects. The KVK network provides training to several hundred thousand farmers each year, but it can cater to the needs of only a miniscule percentage of all farmers. Agricultural education can be moved from the campus into the village by establishing a national network of farm schools, offering practical demonstration and training on lands leased from farmers in the local community. The prime objective of the schools would be to impart knowledge and skills designed to double yields on important commercial crops.

Educated farmers can be trained as self-employed instructors to operate the farm schools as private enterprises on a commercial basis.

Health for All

The health of a nation is difficult to define in terms of a single set of measures. At best, we can assess the health of the population by taking into account indicators like infant mortality and maternal mortality rates, life expectancy and nutrition, along with the incidence of communicable and non-communicable diseases.

According to these measures, the health of the Indian population has improved dramatically over the past fifty years. Life expectancy has risen from 33 years to 64 years. The infant mortality rate (IMR) has fallen from 148 to 71 per 1000. The crude birth rate (CBR) has declined from 41 to 25 and the crude death rate (CDR) has fallen from 25 to under 9. The couple protection rate (CPR) and total fertility rate (TFR) have also improved substantially.

Despite these achievements, wide disparities persist between different income groups, between rural and urban communities, and between different states and even districts within states. The infant mortality rate among the poorest quintet of the population is 2.5 times higher than that among the richest. Maternal mortality remains very high. More than one lakh women die each year due to pregnancy-related complications.

Like population growth and economic growth, the health of a nation is a product of many factors and forces that combine and interact with each other. Economic growth, per capita income, employment, levels of literacy and education — especially among females — age of marriage, birth rates, availability of information regarding health care and nutrition, access to safe drinking water, public and private health care infrastructure, access to preventive health care and medical care, health insurance, public hygiene, road safety, and environmental pollution are among the factors that contribute directly to the health of the nation.

Communicable diseases such as malaria, kalaazar, tuberculosis and HIV infection remain the major causes of illness in India. During the next five to ten years, existing programmes are likely to eliminate polio and leprosy and substantially reduce the prevalence of kalaazar and filariasis. However, TB, malaria and AIDS will continue to remain major public health problems. India has about 1.5 million identified cases of TB that are responsible for more than 3,00,000 deaths annually. Improved diagnostic services and treatment can reduce the prevalence and incidence of TB by 2020. About 2 million cases of malaria are reported in India each year. Restructuring the "malaria workforce" and strengthening health infrastructure can reduce the incidence of this disease by up to 50 per cent within a decade. Assessing the impact of HIV epidemic is more difficult; according to an estimate, there are about 4 million persons infected with HIV. The National Health Policy aims at achieving a plateau in the prevalence of HIV infection by 2007.

Childhood diarrhoea, another major cause of illness, is largely preventable through simple community action and public education, and deaths due to diarrhoea can be eliminated by 2010. Childhood under-nutrition, the other major area of concern, can be addressed by targeting children of low birth weights and employing low-cost screening procedures to detect under-nutrition at an early age. Given the projected improvement in living standards, food security, educational levels and access to health care among all levels of the general population, substantial progress can be made in reducing the prevalence of severe under-nutrition in children by 2020. China's remarkable success in combating disease over the past two decades is proof that a determined commitment to improving public health can dramatically reduce the incidence of infectious diseases within one or two decades.

With the demographic and epidemiological transition taking place in the coming years, non-communicable diseases are also likely to emerge as major public health problems. Modernisation of life styles will further aggravate health problems. The rapid proliferation of two and four wheel motor vehicles, increasing congestion on city roads and intercity highways have all contributed to an increasing number of deaths and serious injuries from traffic related accidents. Greater emphasis on education and enforcement of road safety rules by both drivers and pedestrians is an urgent need of the hour.

As already noted, there will be a massive increase in population in the 15-64 age group. Reproductive and Child Health care programmes must meet the needs of this rapidly growing clientele.

The population in this age group will be more literate and have greater access to information. They will have greater awareness and expectations about access to quality services for maternal and child health, contraceptive care, management of gynaecological problems, etc. A major focus of vision 2020 must be on improving access to health services to meet the health care needs of women and children.

India's significant achievements in the field of health have been made possible by the establishment of a huge rural health infrastructure, along with the formation of a massive health care manpower consisting of over five lakh trained doctors working under plural systems of medicine, and a vast frontline of over seven lakh nurses and other health care workers; 25,000 primary and community health care centres; and 1.6 lakh sub-centres, complemented by 22,000 dispensaries and 2,800 hospitals practicing Indian systems of medicine and homeopathy. This infrastructure remains under-equipped, under-manned and under-financed to cope with the challenge of eradicating major threats to human life.

The inadequacy of the current health care system is starkly illustrated by the fact that only 35 per cent of the population have access to essential drugs, while the UMI reference level is above 82 per cent. Infant immunisation against measles and DPT for children under 12 years is only 60 per cent and 78 per cent compared to the UMI level of over 90 per cent for both diseases.

As a larger proportion of the population reaches middle class standards of living, an increasing number of people will turn to private health care providers. This development is welcome, because it will permit the public health care system to concentrate more resources on meeting the needs of the poorer sections. But at the same time, the level of public expenditure on health care needs to rise about four-fold from the current level of 0.8 per cent of GDP to reach the UMI reference level of 3.4 per cent. Rapid growth of the private health care system, however, requires the formulation of competence and quality standards to check and balance the increasing emphasis on health care as a business.

Criteria for a More Equitable and Effective Health Care System

- Universal access and access to an adequate level of health care without financial burden.
- Fair distribution of financial costs for access and fair distribution of burden in rational care and capacity.
- Ensuring that providers have the competence, empathy and accountability for delivering quality care and for effective use of relevant research.
- Special attention to vulnerable groups such as women, children, the disabled and the aged.

Development plans for India's health care systems need to place greater emphasis on public health education and prevention. The wide dissemination of health and nutrition related information through traditional channels should be supplemented by an ambitious and persistent programme of public health education through the print, television, radio and electronic media.

Health insurance can play an invaluable role in improving the overall health care system. The insurable population in India has been assessed at 250 million and this number will increase rapidly in the coming two decades. This should be supplemented by innovative insurance products and programmes by panchayats with reinsurance backup by companies and government to extend coverage to much larger sections of the population.

The life expectancy of the Indian population is expected to reach above 65 years in 2020, which compares favourably with the UMI reference level of 69 years. Mortality rates for infants is expected to decline to about 20 per 1000 in 2020, which compares favourably with the UMI reference level of 22.5.

Vulnerability

Economic growth, rising levels of education among the young, expansion of employment opportunities for the working age population, slower population growth, and declining infant mortality, however, will not eliminate and may even aggravate, inequalities between different age groups, the sexes, income groups, communities and regions, unless specific corrective steps are taken for levelling the different degrees of capacity and opportunity. The Vision 2020 must have special focus on bridging the existing gaps in the various levels of development and endeavour its best to fulfil the Constitutional commitment of raising the status of the vulnerable groups vis-a-vis the rest of the society.

During the next 20 years, the aged population in India will nearly double, placing much greater demand on the infrastructure of hospitals and nursing homes, while at the same time shifting the profile of health disorders from problems of the young to those of the aged. The population above 65 years of age will increase from 45 to 76 million persons by 2020. Reference has already been made to the very high incidence of malnutrition among this group and the growing incidence of diseases associated with aging, such as cancer and cardiovascular diseases. A disproportionate number of the aged population are illiterate and living below the poverty line. While majority of these people live in rural areas where the extended family system remains prevalent, increasing urbanisation and mobility will destabilise their situation in future. The problem of coping with a larger aged population will be partially solved by a big surge in the size of the working age labour force and a reduction in the dependency ratio, meaning that there will be a larger proportion of workers to support the aged. Specific strategies will be needed to provide targeted assistance for the most vulnerable members of this group, including research on the disabilities of the aged, greater development of geriatric medicine, training of minders for the aged, and establishment of innovative support systems such as the highly successful Japanese model.

Like the aged, the disabled persons also form another subgroup that is particularly vulnerable and unlikely to benefit directly from the general advance of society, unless specific provisions are made to address their particular needs, including a special system of schools, clinics and home-based learning programmes, combined with therapeutic and institutional care.

Increasing gender equity is an important challenge of the coming years. Literacy rates for females are 40 per cent lower than for males. Females represent only 43 per cent of all students at primary level, 37 per cent at higher secondary level, and 35 per cent of those in higher education. Drop out rates are also higher for girls. The UNDP's gender development index ranks India 108th among 174 countries in terms of gender equity. It is no coincidence therefore that countries ranking highest on this index are among the most prosperous in the world. Gender equity and social development are inseparably interlinked. Reducing the disparity in nutritional, literacy and educational levels between the sexes is essential for realisation of the country's full potentials.

Children being the supreme assets of the country, the 'Rights' based approach will continue to play an important role in ensuring their 'survival', 'protection' and 'development', with special attention to the girl child. *Our vision for 2020 in this regard is to see a nation free from all forms of child labour.* However, complete elimination of child labour through legal means is not only difficult to implement but may also prove to be counter productive in protecting the interest of these very children. While legal enforcement can contain the demand for child labour, it may leave the poor households supplying child labour more vulnerable rather than addressing the underlying socio-economic compulsions generating the supply of such labour. Indeed, poverty eradication combined with educational reforms to provide free (or affordable) access to quality education with an interesting, innovative and job-oriented curriculum for all can effectively eliminate child labour once and for all.

The other categories of the vulnerable groups include the scheduled castes (SC), scheduled tribes (ST), other backward classes (OBC) and minorities, constituting nearly three-fourths of the country's total population. They require special attention in order to narrow down the disparities between them and the more privileged section of the population. Literacy rates for SCs and STs are 25 per cent lower than for other communities. Education enrolment rates among this group, especially for females, lag significantly behind that of other communities. Low levels of education lead to lower paying employment opportunities and lower incomes. Thus, it becomes exceedingly difficult for these communities to come out of the vicious circle. Large number of people in other communities also suffer from similar disparities.

Regional disparities in rates of development are of similar concern. Regardless of the community or the region, the overall progress of the nation will depend to a large extent on its ability to provide increasing opportunities for the disadvantaged to take initiative for their self-development. Otherwise, these disadvantaged will exact an increasing toll on the stability, well-being and development of the country as a whole. It is notable that rising levels of violence and crime in society are not so much associated with overall low levels of development, as they are with wide disparities between levels of development, which create frustration and resentment. The progress of the whole will ultimately depend on the progress of its weakest links. *India's Vision of 2020 must be one in which all levels and sections of the population and all parts of the country march forward together into a more secure and prosperous future.*

4

Infrastructure

Urban Development

Disparities between the social and physical infrastructure of the urban and rural areas are common to all countries. In India they are a continuing source of concern and will become further aggravated unless innovative strategies are evolved to accelerate the development of rural infrastructure. A Vision of India 2020 must assess and try to anticipate the complexion of the future urban-rural divide.

Recent evidence confirms that the rate of growth of urban centres in the country is declining more rapidly than was previously anticipated, though the proportion of people living in urban areas continues to rise. According to the 2001 Census, 27.8 per cent of the Indian population reside in cities, compared with 25.5 per cent in 1990. The urban population is expected to rise to around 40 per cent by 2020. As India's cities continue to swell, the challenge of improving the urban infrastructure will be magnified. For instance, only 73 per cent of India's urban population has access to improved sanitation facilities, compared to the UMI reference level of 95 per cent.

The trend towards concentration of urban population in a small number of large urban centres has been taking shape over a century. While the number of urban centres doubled between 1901 and 1991, the urban population increased eight-fold, resulting in a top heavy urban hierarchy. Future demographic and economic growth is likely to concentrate in and around 60 to 70 large cities in the country having a population of a million people or more.

The demographic trends towards urbanisation are accompanied by a change in the management and financing of urban development as a result of liberalisation. Decentralisation of municipal governance has led to a substantial reduction in budgetary allocations for infrastructural development. Greater reliance is now placed on institutional financing and capital markets for resource mobilisation and on private companies for service delivery.

Disparities in infrastructure between large and small urban areas have always been prevalent, but these disparities can be expected to increase significantly in future years. The stricter fiscal disciplines imposed by government and credit rating agencies will make it increasingly difficult for all but the largest urban centres to attract finance for infrastructural development. The large cities may be expected to experience modest to high rates of growth and to absorb a large part of the incremental migration in their peripheries and neighbouring towns. Being linked to the national and global economy, these large areas are likely to attract investment from the corporate sector and experience a stable demographic growth, while small and medium towns, particularly in backward regions, attract little industrial and infrastructural investment and report low and unstable demographic growth. This almost exclusive focus on improving infrastructure and basic amenities in the large cities is misplaced. Still greater inequality may be expected in the level of basic services across urban centres of different sizes by the year 2020, unless concerted initiative is taken to reverse the trend.

The gross inadequacies of infrastructure, especially those of public transport, water supply and sanitation, demand corrective action. A strategy for developing capabilities within the urban local bodies to cope with the infrastructural deficiencies must be adopted, with genuine decentralisation of financial and administrative powers and restructuring of the entities on the basis of sound management practices.

The face of urban poverty in 2020 is unlikely to be very different from what it is today, given that the largest indicator of poverty in cities is not so much lack of income, as lack of decent housing and civic amenities. These call for a change in a number of policies, especially those relating to land regulation, zoning, and development. The activities relating to provision of health care, water supply and sanitation, education and vocational training need to be carried out with higher levels of efficiency, to help the urban poor upgrade themselves.

While improving infrastructure in existing cities/towns is not to be ignored, in the next two decades there will be need to encourage growth of new townships and take up regional urban development plans where growth corridors can be identified and public-private partnerships promoted for investment in alternative nodes of development. Such centres will have considerable impact in improving the urban profile of the country. They will, however, need to make provision for adequate supply of water and sanitation as well as other civic amenities. They will also need to chalk out more liberal policies towards education and health care in order to attract a cosmopolitan group of investors, professionals and providers of other services. While a large part of it will cater to the affluent, through imaginative planning the new centres can serve the needs of the hinterland also by offering avenues for employment, housing and other needs of a large workforce.

Urban development represents one of the great challenges for India over the next two decades. Given the socio-political reality in India, it will be difficult for the private sector to bring about changes in the pattern of investment in infrastructure without the state becoming an active partner, bringing about the required legislative and administrative changes. A satisfying outcome will depend on the formulation of effective public policy to accelerate all-round development of smaller urban centres and to refashion the role of the state as an effective facilitator to compensate for the deficiencies of market mechanisms in the delivery of public goods. Anti-poverty programmes should primarily be directed towards creation of a community-based infrastructure.

Rural Infrastructure

Along with the development of urban infrastructure, simultaneous efforts are also needed for strengthening rural infrastructure. Specific aspects of the rural infrastructure are discussed elsewhere in this report under the headings of education, health care, transport, telecom, power and water. Our vision is to create a rural infrastructure which connects every village with paved roads and telecommunication facilities, provides electricity and an assured supply of safe drinking water to all rural households, offers access to quality primary and secondary education to all children and medical services to all citizens.

The rural electrification programme, launched in 1951, has succeeded in bringing electricity to more than 5 lakh villages. However, 80,000 villages are yet to get electricity connections. Out of these, 18,000 are in remote areas where electrification through the conventional electricity grid may not be feasible. To achieve 100 per cent rural electrification, we must rely on non-conventional sources of energy, especially for the remote villages. A detailed discussion regarding the potential for such energy sources is given elsewhere in this report.

But the problem of rural infrastructure cannot be viewed or tackled in terms of a composite of separate services or in isolation from changes affecting the urban landscape. A comprehensive and integrated strategy is required. The future development of urban centres will widen the disparities in civic infrastructure that exist between urban and rural communities, thereby stimulating greater migration to the cities and rapid expansion of urban slum areas. The natural growth of urban areas will make this trend inevitable unless bold steps are taken to promote an alternative, more geographically dispersed and equitable development paradigm. Past efforts to develop satellite townships and growth centres in the vicinity of large cities have mitigated the concentration of population in central urban business districts to some extent, but in the process it has furthered the concentration of population in mega cities.

Rural livings offer several considerable advantages over their urban counterparts: However, any successful alternative approach must address the crucial issues of infrastructure and civic amenities that make urban areas so attractive.

Comparative Advantages

Urban

- Domestic services: piped water, electricity, telecommunications and sanitation.
- Primary or localised services: shops, dispensaries, and playgrounds.
- Secondary services: schools, police stations, railway, fire-fighting services, and hospitals, which need not be local but must be readily accessible when required.
- Tertiary services: airports, wholesale markets, referral hospitals, etc. which are less frequently demanded.

Rural

- Living space is much cheaper and more abundant.
- The environment is much healthier.
- Commuting times between work and home are much shorter.

One promising alternative is to link clusters of ten villages together by a high speed circular highway, thereby bringing 100,000 or more people into a circular community that can be crossed within 30 minutes travel time, and promoting a balanced and well spread out development of urban services along the periphery of the ring road. This arrangement would vastly reduce the length and cost of constructing good roads between all the villages, and enable establishment of quality services at any point around the ring to be accessible to all members of the linked community. Telecom links and sanitation systems would naturally develop around the ring at far lower cost, and better quality schools and hospitals could develop to support the larger community. Industrial parks could be established to utilise the large workforce available within the ring. These and similar models need to be tried and modified, on a priority basis, otherwise it requires little stretch of imagination to anticipate the increasing congestion and immobility of large urban areas that is bound to occur in the near future.

Telecom

Telecom acts as a stimulus for the development process. Over the past decade, India's achievement in this sector has been quite impressive. In terms of the overall size of main telephone lines in operation, the country rose from its 14th rank in the world in 1995 to 7th in 2001.

India has adopted a gradual approach towards telecom sector reforms, through selective privatisation and managed competition in different market segments. Since the early 1990s, it has introduced private competition in value-added services, and national and international long distance telephony. Two state-owned public sector incumbents with a large existing subscriber base still dominate the fixed line service, in which they own about 35 million direct exchange lines (DEL). While the number of DELs has multiplied six-fold since 1991, demand for new lines has grown nearly as fast, resulting in persistent shortfall of supply and a current waiting list of nearly 3 million lines. India has also achieved significant quality upgradation of its network in the 1990s, achieving almost 100 per cent conversion to digital lines. At the same time there has been a significant reduction in telecom rates paid by consumers.

The opening up of the cellular market has unleashed real dynamism in the marketplace. Cellular mobile telephone subscribers in India increased from 77 thousand in 1995 to 7.3 million by June 2002, rising from a 0.6 per cent of the total subscribers to 17 per cent. This level is still relatively low compared with the average level of about 25 per cent achieved by low-income countries, 42 per cent by middle-income countries, and upwards of 50 per cent by upper middle-income and high-income countries. The mobile explosion is helping in improving telecom penetration, bringing along the concomitant economic benefits of enhanced telecom accessibility, while at the same time promoting a better entrepreneurial culture, generating additional employment, and fostering a shift in the investment burden from the state to the private sector and the consumers.

Table – 6

Number of Main Telephone Lines per 100 Inhabitants

Country	2001
USA	66.45
Germany	63.48
Japan	59.69
UK	57.78
France	57.35
Korea, Rep.	47.60
Russia	24.33
Turkey	28.52
Brazil	21.69
China	13.81
India	3.38

Source: Manas Bhattacharya: "Telecom Sector in India: Vision 2020", Paper prepared for Planning Commission.

In spite of a significant expansion of capacity, however, India's tele-density remains appallingly low, as shown in Table 6, and closing the digital divide in terms of tele-density remains a daunting task. In order to attain the current network size of UMI countries by 2020, India will have to increase the number of telephone lines seven-fold in 18 years.

Targeted intervention through access promotion can be an important strategy for achieving growth with greater equity. The launching of private franchises for public call offices (PCOs) handling both domestic and long distance services has resulted in an increase in the number of PCOs from 0.2 million in 1993 to 0.9 million in 2001, including 0.4 million in villages. The presence of the private sector is widespread in PCOs and Internet Kiosks in the cities and towns, but remains insignificant in rural areas which account for only about 23 per cent of the country's fixed phone lines. The aggressive expansion of public sector telecommunications infrastructure in geographically remote parts of the country, where private industry cannot venture profitably, is essential for unleashing the latent economic energies and market forces in these regions.

Looking forward from now to 2020, the rapid expansion of India's fixed line network is likely to continue. As the fixed line market matures, more and more users will cross over to mobile communications as well, spurring a mobile revolution in India. Mobile telecommunications and the Internet are going to set the contours of further technological progress over the next two decades. The recent convergence of voice and data transmission, global satellite systems, mobile handsets and calling cards have overcome the technological barriers of distance, topography and remoteness. By 2020, third generation (3G) mobile devices with access to mobile data and voice should be within the reach of wider sections of the Indian population.

The last decade also witnessed a phenomenal growth in the use of Internet. Private Internet service providers have been allowed to set up international Internet gateways, as well as both satellite and landing stations for submarine optical fiber cables. Internet telephony is also opening up. India must strive to complete the transition into digital switching and transmission, voice over Internet protocol (VoIP), broadband and 3G by 2020.

Despite differences across countries, the global trend is towards growing privatisation and competition in telecommunications. Global experience suggests that this process is likely to undergo alternating cylces of differentiation and convergence. The convergent nature of technology may dictate mergers and acquisitions between companies in certain cases. Network operators and service providers may have to merge with content developers to add value to their services. This may create temporary conditions of oligopoly until the emergence of new firms, offering multiple services, intensifies competition. India in 2020 is likely to see competition among big firms offering innovative value-added services to capture market share. The regulatory environment should therefore forster maximum flexibility and freedom to encourage innovation and expansion, consistent with this process of evolution.

Rapid flow of information is a catalyst for social development. Vision 2020 conceives of India evolving into an information society and knowledge economy built on the edifice of information and communication technology (ICT), of which telecommunications is the springboard. Telecom is improving opportunities for people across different social strata. A whole range of information-based industries and applications have come up, creating new sources of employment and earnings with welfare enhancing consequences for both the poor and the wealthy. As a metatechnology, ICT has caused rapid innovations to occur in other areas of material sciences. It has improved access in the fields of education, healthcare, governance and business services. It has also enhanced the ability of the poor to manage risks and mitigate vulnerabilities through provision of timely information. Rapid expansion and extension of the country's fixed and mobile telecom infrastructure is essential for stimulating growth of both the ICT sector and the economy as a whole.

Transport

Development involves a continuous increase in the number of physical transactions and the speed with which they occur, both of which are highly dependent on the size and quality of the nation's transport system. India's network of roads, railways, air services and ports is one of the largest in the world, serving a land mass of 3.3 million square km and a population of over one billion. Over the last 50 years, the growth of this network and of the demand for transport services has been enormous. The volume of railway freight has increased five-fold and passenger kilometers nearly seven-fold. The length of surfaced roads has multiplied nine-fold. The number of goods vehicles has increased 40-fold, buses 20-fold and four-wheel passenger vehicles 30-fold. The tonnage of freight handled by the nation's expanding system of major and minor ports has grown more than 16-fold. Air-freight tonnage has increased about 30-fold.

Currently, about 800 billion tonne km of freight and 2,3000 billion passenger km are handled by the transport system, with the total transport demand growing at around 10 per cent a year for the past decade. The modal growth rates have varied, with road transport and air services growing at a much faster rate than the railways. The relative share of railways in total freight and passenger traffic has declined dramatically over the past five decades, from 90 to 25 per cent of inland freight and from 75 to 18 per cent of inland passenger. Meanwhile, the share of road transport has increased from 12 to 60 per cent of freight and from 32 to 80 per cent of passenger business.

Growing urbanisation is a natural phenomenon and despite all its implications has beneficial effects on economic growth. Increasing population combined with continued urbanisation are likely to raise India's urban population to around 540 million over the next two decades, resulting in the emergence of about 60 to 70 cities with population of more than a million. Lack of adequate public transport has resulted in a rapid increase in private ownership of vehicles, particularly two wheelers, with consequent adverse effects of air and noise pollution. In most cities, two wheelers comprise more than 70 per cent of total motor vehicles. Based on current growth rates, two-wheeler ownership in cities with more than 100,000 inhabitants is likely to rise from 102 to 393 per thousand population in the next 20 years, while the number of cars increases from 14 to 48 per thousand.

To contain this explosion of personal vehicle movement in cities, massive investment in mass transport services will become necessary. Public investment in transport has declined steadily over the past four decades from 23 per cent of the total plan funds in 1960 to around 12 per cent in the 1980s and 1990s. Considering the developing nature of the country and the deficiencies in its transport system, a larger proportion of resources will need to be invested in improvements to the transport infrastructure.

Among the most daunting problems faced by India's cities are the inadequate public transport infrastructure, long travel times and high transport cost for both passenger and goods traffic. The growth of cities has been haphazard, expanding around a compact central core with industrialisation and migration bringing about rapid change in peripheral land use, resulting in urban sprawl. No organised, viable and significant public transport system is available in major cities, except the four metro areas of Mumbai, Kolkata, Chennai and Delhi. Bus and rail systems are the mainstay of public transport in these cities. Transport planning must go hand-in-hand with land use planning. Specific plans will need to be formulated by each urban authority, starting with the provision of bus services, developing intermediate public transport and identifying corridors for future growth, including reserving land for such activity.

In the long run, rail-based mass transport systems appear to be the only viable solution to the problems of urban transport in India's major metropolitan areas. Where flexibility of land use is possible, electrified surface rail transport can be adopted. In the case of highly developed and congested areas, underground or flyover systems will have to be considered. On medium density corridors, electric trolley buses or CNG operated buses may be best suited.

A key component of rural development is the provision of roads for connectivity, access being essential for social and economic well-being. Families residing along side roads benefit from better health, greater educational opportunities, smaller sized families and higher ownership of assets, compared to those families living in remote villages. While almost all villages with population above 1,500 are now connected by road, more than 45 per cent of villages with less than 1,000 people still need to be connected. There are also significant regional imbalances in the connectivity of villages. Poor road maintenance is a related problem. The Government has allocated resources to achieve all-weather road access to all villages with population above 1,000 by 2003, and for villages with population between 500 and 1,000 by 2007.

While the progress made in the transport sector has been significant, it has not been able to meet the growing demand, particularly in the last decade when economic reforms triggered an unprecedented growth of GDP. Efforts to achieve even higher GDP growth rates in future years cannot be sustained without correspondingly greater efforts to strengthen the nation's transport system. The existing issues and concerns, the congestion and constraints in movement leading to higher transport costs, and other unfinished tasks will be some of the challenges that need to be met during the next two decades. A huge increase in demand for both railways and road transport will require not only massive investments but also modification in pricing policies, increasing customer focus, improved terminal management, enhanced safety, reduced transit times, and other changes required to provide adequate and efficient services for meeting the growth in demand and public expectations.

Based on projected GDP growth of 8 per cent per annum, the total freight traffic is likely to reach about 5,500 billion tonne km by the year 2020, five times the level in year 2000. If a 10 per cent growth is achieved, the traffic demand would exceed 10,000 billion tonne km. Assuming that railways retain a 20 per cent market share, rail freight traffic, measured in tonne km, will increase three to six-fold. The proportion of manufactured products to bulk cargo will also rise, with a larger proportion of liquids being carried through the pipelines. General merchandise will travel longer distances and in much smaller consignments, favouring smaller carrying units. The rising value of consignments will place a higher premium on the speed of transit in order to minimise inventories. The total logistical management of transportation, marketing and distribution will become commonplace for most general merchandise. These changes, together with the impact of other factors such as energy efficiency, environmental pollution, and technological changes in each mode, will result in changing preferences for alternative modes of transport.

Passenger traffic is expected to increase more than four-fold over the next 20 years. For long distance travel, the demand for air services will grow rapidly, as speed becomes an increasingly important consideration. Already more people travel between Delhi and Mumbai by air than by rail. Overnight sleeper class travel will continue to be the railways' strength, as long as booking, reservations, comfort and other customer services are continuously enhanced to keep pace with rising customer expections.

For medium distances up to 500 kms — with four-lane highways connecting the country, expressways coming up close to the main metro cities, and car ownership increasing rapidly — the bulk of the passenger travel may start moving towards 'own vehicle travel', a phenomenon already observed in most countries. Fast inter-city rail services will have an edge over air travel for this segment of traffic.

Road transport is best suited for short distance traffic, except where volumes increase to very high levels and rail-based mass rapid transport offers a cost-effective alternative.

Future Trends in Transport

- Improvement in the length, quality and speed of transport networks.
- Increase in productivity and economic efficiency of transport.
- Higher frequency and quality of services.
- Better control of air and noise pollution.
- Increased mobility for commuters, business and recreational travel.
- Improved urban transport systems.
- Corresponding improvements in rural transport.
- Fewer transport constraints to trade.
- Reduced transport transit times in general and at initial loading and terminal points.
- Better energy efficiency.
- Improved safety with fewer accidents.

Our vision of India 2020 is of a country with a well-developed network of roads and railways and adequate capacity to handle the growth in demand for transport. The volume of road traffic will multiply about five-fold, carried over a 70,000 km network of National Highways, including 5,000 to 10,000 km of expressways, linking the golden quadrangle of Delhi-Mumbai-Chennai-Kolkata-Delhi as well as northern, southern, eastern and western portions of the country, mostly with four or more lanes. State Highways with at least two ways lanes will link most districts. Rural roads will provide access to the furthest outlying villages. Technological progress will generate vehicles that are pollution free and fuel-efficient. An efficient public transport system will lead to a reduction in the population of two-wheelers in major urban areas.

The railways will have to be expanded to handle a three-fold increase in traffic. Improved customer service, comfort and safety, a reduction in freight costs and tariffs, elimination (or at least reduction) of the uneconomic services, non-paying projects and subsidies will be necessary for this. India will need airports of international standards for passenger and cargo handling and modern handling systems at major ports to reduce delays in berthing. Institutional arrangements will need to be in placc with adequate funds for proper maintenance, especially of roads. Urban transport systems will be needed in all cities with a population of a million plus.

We envisage that connection of several distributaries of the rivers through a network of canals will give impetus to the development of inland water transport.

Investment requirements to meet these needs will increase to levels three to four times higher than the present in real terms. While the government will continue to be a major source of funds for infrastructure, internal generation of resources by the transport services will have to increase, supported by more realistic pricing of transport services and reduction in operating costs. The private sector will need to play a more central role in the development and operation of transport systems.

5

Energy and the Environment

Economic growth the world over is driven by energy, whether in the form of finite resources such as coal, oil and gas or in renewable forms such as hydroelectric, wind, solar and biomass, or its converted form, electricity. This energy generation and consumption powers the nation's industries, vehicles, homes and offices. It also has significant impact on the quality of the country's air, water, land and forest resources. For future growth to be both rapid and sustainable, it needs to be as resource-efficient and environmentally benign as possible.

Power

India's installed capacity for power generation has tripled over the last 20 years and now exceeds 101,000 MW. However, the total demand is expected to increase by another 3.5 times in the next two decades, even under a best-case scenario that envisions intensified efforts to modernise power plants, improve transmission and distribution efficiency, and adopt more efficient generation technologies. Figure 2 depicts power consumption by various sectors in 1997 compared to a business-as-usual (BAU) and an alternative scenario which we will consider as the best-case scenario (BCS) for 2020.

Figure – 2

Projected Power Demand (TWh)

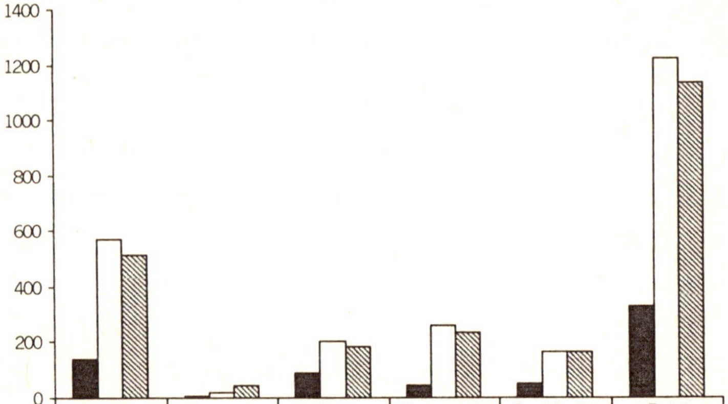

	Industry	Transport	Agriculture	Commercial	Residential	Total
■ 1997	137	7	89	47	48	329
□ BAU 2020	570	22	202	262	165	1221
▧ BCS 2020	510	45	181	235	163	1134

Source: Based on R.K. Pachauri and Pooja Mehrotra, "Vision 2020: Sustainability of our Material Resources", paper prepared for Planning Commission.

The soaring demand for power will necessitate a tripling of the installed generation capacity from 101,000 to 292,000 MW over the next two decades. The projected fuel mix for power generation from various sources is shown in Figure 3. At least two-thirds of this power will have to come from thermal sources — coal, oil and gas — even under the BCS. This will mean a spiralling cost for imported fuels, including coal, since even a doubling of domestic coal production would not be sufficient to meet the demand. It will also mean a surge in emission of environmental pollutants. Even under this alternative scenario, the contribution of renewable energy does not exceed 5 per cent of the total production.

Figure – 3

Fuel Mix for Power Generation (TWh)

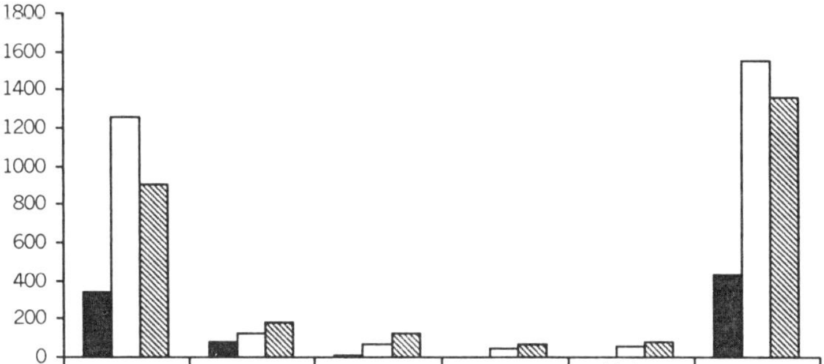

	Thermal	Hydro	Nuclear	Renewables	Hydro (Import)	Total
■ 1997	336	75	10	4	1	426
□ BAU 2020	1259	119	70	49	54	1551
▧ BCS 2020	911	181	127	68	76	1363

Source: Same as Figure 2

Fuel Demand

The overall growth in demand for all forms of fuel will mirror the growth in the power sector. Even under the alternative scenario, total coal demand will nearly double, and both oil and gas demand will triple, as shon in Table 7. Expanding domestic production capacity will require substantial investments, while increasing dependence on imported forms of energy will increase vulnerability to fluctuations in global energy prices. The surging demand will also place an increased burden on the physical and social environments. An enhanced exploration by the public and private sectors, adoption of best practices and environment-friendly technologies, more efficient use of energy, promotion of private sector investment, and greater efforts to protect the environment will be required to cope effectively with the nation's growing energy needs.

Table – 7

Projected Fuel Demand

	Coal (million tons)	Oil (millions tons)	Gas (billion cubic mtrs)
1997	311	83	21.5
2020 BAU	688	245	70.8
2020 BCS	538	195	64.7

Source: Same as Figure 2.

The growth in demand for oil depicted in Figure 4 shows that the largest increases will be for transportation and industry. Domestic oil production has remained relatively constant over the past decade, while oil imports have more than doubled. If the BAU scenario depicted in Table 7 were to be realised, it would require a more than tripling of oil imports. Even under the BCS, oil imports would have to increase two-fold.

Figure – 4

Projected Demand for Oil

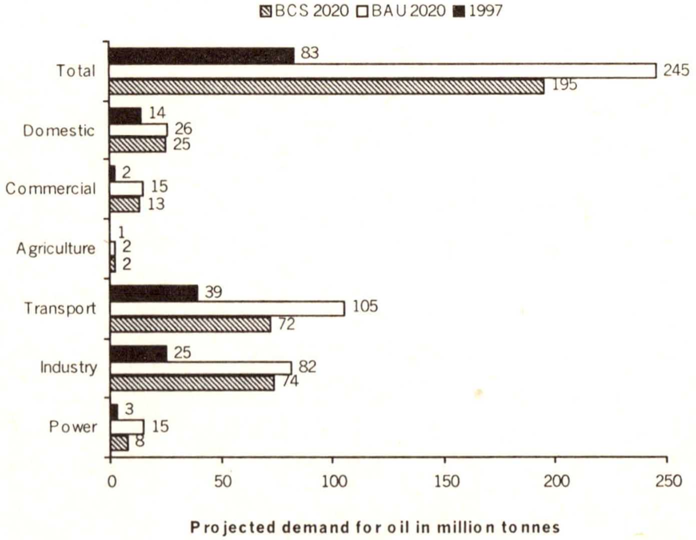

Source: Same as Figure 2

Long-term forecasts for the price of oil are at best precarious. A recent forecast by the Institute of Energy Economics of Japan shows the price fluctuating within a band from $ 17 to $ 23 per barrel over the next 20 years.

The growth in demand for natural gas depicted in Figure 5 shows that the largest increases willl be for power and industry, especially fertilisers. Domestic gas production is expected to meet around 20 per cent of the total demand, thereby requiring massive import of gas. Plans for gas pipeline projects from Bangladesh and Iran as well as LNG terminals along India's coastlines are already being contemplated.

Figure – 5

Projected Demand for Natural Gas

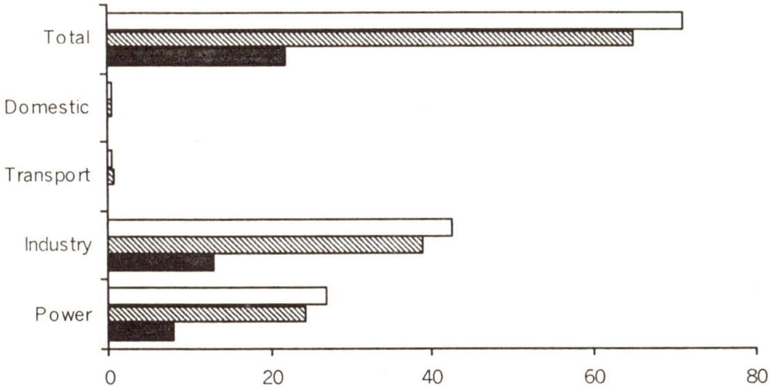

	Power	Industry	Transport	Domestic	Total
□ BAU 2020	27	42.6	0.5	0.6	71
▧ BCS 2020	24.3	39	0.9	0.5	65
■ 1997	8.1	13.1	0.1	0.2	22

Projected demand for gas in billion cubic meters

Source: Same as Figure 2

The alternative scenario for oil and gas presents a combination of technological developments, governance measures, and market-based instruments that will reduce resource requirements. It places greater reliance on gas for environmental considerations. The spread of cleaner technologies among transport vehicles should lead to improved air quality in the cities.

Renewable Energy

Greater reliance on renewable energy sources offers enormous economic, social and environmental benefits. India is already the world's fifth largest producer of wind power, with more than 95 per cent of the investment coming from the private sector. Other renewable energy technologies, including solar photovoltaic, solar thermal, small hydro and biomass power are also spreading. Under the BAU scenario the contribution of renewable forms of energy is expected to be quite modest, but a concerted effort to implement a more visionary plan could significantly alter this outcome. Apart from reducing India's dependence on imported fuels and the strain on the environment, some forms of renewable energy such as biomass power production and ethanol motor fuel offer the added advantage of potentially creating millions of rural employment opportunities and contributing to higher rural incomes, rather than higher outflows of foreign exchange. Tapping this potential will require conducive national policies and programmes designed to attract active participation from the private sector.

However, a far more aggressive alternative scenatio is also possible in which the country makes a massive commitment to the development of biomass power, biogas and biofuels that could act as a powerful stimulus to rural job-creation and prosperity, while radically reducing India's dependence on imported fuels. (See box)

Biomass Power & Bio-fuels for Rural Job-creation & Prosperity

India has approximately 50 million hectares of degraded wasteland that lie outside the areas demarcated as national forests, and another 34 million hectares of protected forest area, in much of which tree cover is severely degraded. A massive programme to develop energy plantations consisting of fast-growing tree crops such as Bamboo, Casuarina and Eucalyptus can serve as the raw material for a national network of small, decentralised biomass power plants. These power plants, ranging in size from 10-25 MW, can generate thousands of megawatts of power from renewable, forest-based fuel sources in a cost-effective manner. This would reduce India's dependence on imported fuel oils, stimulate private investment in the power sector, and generate massive income and employment opportunities for the rural poor. Establishment of 40 million hectares of energy plantation would be sufficient to generate 100,000 MW of power and provide year-round employment for 30 million people.

India also has the capacity to generate biofuels in massive quantities. Curcas (*jatropha curcas*) is a plant introduced from Africa, which already grows wild in India. The plant produces large quantities of seeds which contain up to 35 per cent oil that is a substitute for No. 2 diesel and kerosene and can be blended in diesel motor fuels up to 15 per cent. The cost of production is competitive with other fuel oils. Cultivation of 10 million hectares of this crop could generate 7.5 million tons of fuel annually, while generating year-round employment for 5 million people.

Ethanol, which can be produced from maize, tapioca, sugarcane, sugar beet and other crops, is another biofuel with enormous potential. It can be mixed as a pollution-free blend with petrol and diesel. Ethanol-petrol fuel blends are utilised in more than 20 countries, including Brazil, Canada, Sweden and USA. Between 1979 and 1992, this enabled Brazil to reduce reliance on imported oil by 70 per cent. Introducing 10 per cent ethanol fuel with petrol and diesel could create potential demand for more than 10 million tons of ethanol per annum.

The greatest advantage of biomass power and bio-fuels is that they can generate tens of millions of rural jobs and stimulate enormous growth of rural incomes, especially among the weaker sections. Therefore, these strategies should not be regarded from the narrow perspective of energy alone, but from the wider perspective of national development.

Air Quality

Transport, manufacturing, the power sector, commercial and residential energy use, all contribute to problems of air quality. Motor vehicles contribute to all forms of air pollution. Residential burning of unprocessed biomass fuel is the single largest source of carbon monoxide and suspended particulate matter. Power generation contributes most of the nitrogen oxides and sulphur dioxide.

The escalating demand for power, rapid proliferation of motor vehicles, expansion of industries and rising living standards will all combine to have significant impact on the quality of air, especially in urban areas, as depicted in Figure 6. Appropriate strategies and actions are required to address the various forms of pollution in each of these sectors. Stricter enforcement of environmental regulations, rapid adoption of pollution-free and more efficient technologies, and higher standards for fuel quality are needed to reduce the environmental costs of growth.

Figure – 6

Projected Air Emissions

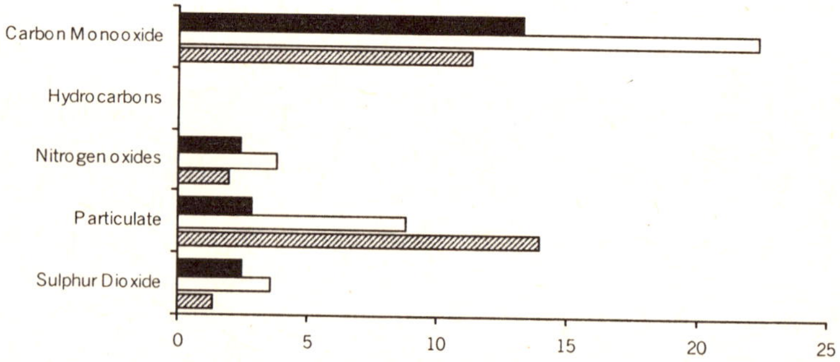

	Sulphur Dioxide	Particulate	Nitrogen oxides	Hydrocarbons	Carbon Monooxide
■ 2020 BCS	2.47	2.83	2.37	0.04	13.27
□ 2020 BAU	3.57	8.82	3.84	0.07	22.32
▨ 1997	1.38	13.93	1.91	0.02	11.33

Projected Emissions in Million Tonnes

Source: Same as Figure 2

Water Management

India possesses 16 per cent of the world's population but just 4 per cent of its water resources. Overall, at the national level, current water resources are more than sufficient to meet the demand, but future studies project that the supply situation could become difficult over the next half century. However, water shortage has already become a serious and recurring source of concern for a large number of people in different parts of the country and for a number of the major metropolitan areas. Only 70 per cent of the people in urban areas have access to basic sanitation services. A large number of rural habitations remain without any identified source of safe drinking water. Groundwater tables are receding, rivers are silting up, and leaching of chemical fertilizers is polluting drinking water supplies.

The rising consumption will further aggravate water scarcity as population, food production, industrialisation and living standards continue to rise over the next two decades. The total water consumption in India is expected to rise by 20-40 per cent over the next 20 years. Figure 7 shows the current and projected consumption of water for different categories of use.

Figure – 7

Projected Water Consumption

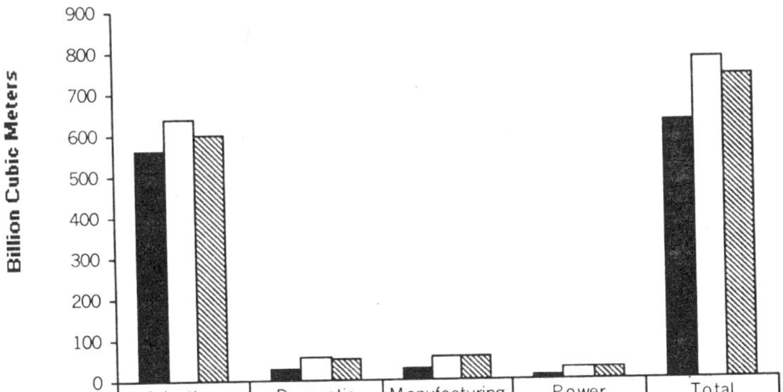

	Irrigation	Domestic	Manufacturing	Power	Total
■ 1997-98	560	30	30	9	629
□ 2020 BAU	640	56	57	28	781
▧ 2020 BCS	602	51	57	27	737

Source: Water Resources Division, Planning Commission

To meet the rising demand for water in 2020, it is essential to develop potential storage capacities and strengthen existing storage facilities. Agriculture accounts for 89 per cent of the total water consumption and domestic consumption accounts for 4.8 per cent. Subsidised or free supply of power and water has resulted in overexploitation and inefficient use of water in agriculture, leading to water-logging and salinity on 5.76 million hectares. Tremendous wastage occurs as a result of evapostranspiration, distribution losses, seepage through unlined channels and excess application. Canal-irrigation efficiency in India is estimated at around 35 to 40 per cent, which is below international standards. Government policies need to be revised to provide incentives for efficient use of water, including appropriate water pricing and more effective institutional mechanisms for water management.

India is not poor in water resources. What it lacks is the ability to efficiently capture and effectively utilise the available resources for the maximum benefit. Enormous potential exists for increasing the productivity of water in agriculture by raising crop productivity, combined with better water management. Deep soil chiseling prior to planting can dramatically improve water retention by the soil, while reducing run-off and flooding. Crops grown in these conditions require less irrigation and generate much higher yields.

Both urban and rural water resources can be substantially enhanced by widespread adoption of rainwater harvesting techniques. These techniques need to be applied throughout the country, in both rural and urban areas, to capture run-off water during the monsoon season and channel it into ponds, tanks and bore wells in order to recharge both surface water and underground aquifers.

A serious degradation in the quality of groundwater and river water has occurred due to excessive and indiscriminate use of pesticides and chemical fertilisers in agriculture, as well as salinity resulting from overexploitation of groundwater. The deterioration of water quaity is compounded by lack of proper effluent treatment for domestic waste water and industrial wastes. Stricter enforcement of environmental regulations is essential for stemming further degradation, and enactment of groundwater legislation is necessary to check over exploitation.

Given the enormous cost of major water projects, emphasis needs to shift from large scale projects for augmenting water supply to decentralised projects designed to manage water demand and conserve water resources. The National Water Policy 2002 advocates an integrated approach to water resources development with a river basin as a planning unit. The Policy emphasises community participation in management of water resources, appropriate pricing for water, tackling of pollution of surface and ground water bodies, and encouragement to the private sector to invest in water resources development. What is now required is to operationalise the policy by preparing state level policies and drawing up action plans to implement the various recommendations.

For the past fifty years, public imagination has been stirred by proposals to link major rivers together in a manner that would channel surpluses from flood-prone areas into drought-prone regions, create millions of hectares of additional irrigated land, provide an inexpensive system of inland water transport, and generate millions of additional employment opportunities in construction, agriculture, trade and industrial development. The high cost estimates of such a system — recent estimates place the cost at more than Rs. 500,000 crores — as well as some technical and political issues involved have been perceived as serious obstacles to implementation. However, the potential benefits to the nation of linking even some of the major rivers, subject to technical feasibility, are so vast that pragmatic proposals demand serious consideration. Given the vision and political will, India can convert the present water problem into a huge opportunity.

Land, Forest and Biodiversity

India's wide range of agro-climatic regions, vast extent of land and forest, and rich variety of biodiversity, rank it among the most naturally endowed nations of the world. But its huge and still expanding human and animal populations and its urge for industrialisation tax these resources to the limit. Competing uses of land for agriculture, forestry, pastures, human settlements and industries exert increasing pressure on the country's finite land resources, influencing land-use patterns and sometimes causing degradation of forests and soils. Changes in land use and land cover, together with land degradation have adverse impacts on forest resources and biodiversity. Increasing demand for forest resources is of particular concern.

Yet the potential exists for dramatically reversing this pattern of degradation during the next two decades. It can be done by a concerted and systematic effort to halt soil erosion, restore precious nutrients and organic material to crop lands, recharge groundwater tables, and re-establish depleted forest lands, together with a holistic approach to land management that combines technologies and policies to integrate ecological, socio-economic, and political principles.

Figure 8 shows current and projected land use pattern under the business-as-usual and alternative scenario. While the amount of land under agriculture remains constant, the quality of that land will be enormously enhanced by the policies and programmes already mentioned. The most significant improvement under the alternative scenario is the increase in land under forest and tree cover from the current level of 71 million hectares to 83 million hectares (See Table 8).

Figure – 8

Projected Land Use

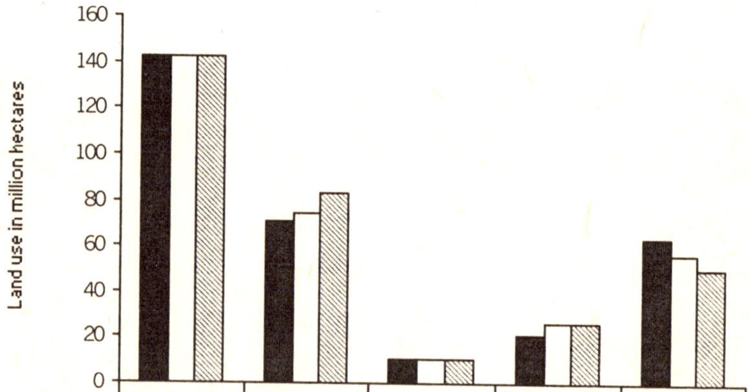

	Agriculture	Forest Cover	Pastures	Settlements & Industry	Wasteland
■ 1997	142	71	11	21	64
□ 2020 BAU	142	74.1	11	26.2	56.7
▧ 2020 BCS	142	83.4	11	26.2	50.6

Source: Same as Figure 2

Table – 8

Projected Land Use - Percentage Distribution

	1997	2020 BAU	2020 BCS
Agriculture	45.9	45.8	45.3
Forest Cover	23.0	23.9	26.6
Pastures	3.5	3.5	3.5
Settlements & Industry	6.8	8.5	8.4
Wasteland	20.7	18.3	16.2

Source: Same as Figure 8

At present, 40 per cent of the commercial demand for timber and less than 20 per cent of the demand for fuel wood are being met by sustainable supply from the forests. Population growth will result in rising demand for both. Over-grazing and over-extraction of green fodder lead to forest degradation through decreased vegetative regeneration, soil compaction and erosion.

Combating the pressure on forests requires a combination of measures. A superior genetic stock is required to correct the poor productivity of Indian forests, which is a third below world averages. Extensive areas should be brought under joint forest management and plantation forestry. Plantation forestry can be expanded through the combined efforts of local communities, NGOs, and the corporate sector, which will provide the technological, financial and organisational resources required, while generating millions of employment opportunities for rural and tribal communities. Removal of legal and technical barriers by rationalising land-ceiling laws, removing restrictions on harvest and sale of timber, and devising incentives to attract private investment are essential for achieving these goals.

The degradation of land and forest is also endangering India's rich biodiversity. Maintaining viable populations of plant and animal species which form the basis for traditional systems of medicine and also hold vast potential for modern science, requires the conservation of important ecosystems, habitats and the ecological processes of which they are a part. While the country has nearly achieved the international goal of reserving 5 per cent of its area as protected, some important biomes and species are not yet covered. This can be accomplished by an expansion of the system of national parks and sanctuaries combined with enhancing control and enforcement of wildlife trade, creation of new conservation reserves, conservation forestry, integration of rural development and biodiversity strategies, and a range of other legal, administrative and technical measures.

6

Globalisation

India's progress over the next 20 years will be intimately linked to events within the region as well as around the world. Both opportunities and challenges will arise as the result of transformations in the regional and global political and security environments. World trade under WTO will determine access to markets and international competitiveness, particularly after the ascension of China. The economic growth rates of other regions will influence demand for exports and foreign capital flows. Some other developments that will influence India's progress in the coming two decades are: pressure on energy prices as a result of global economic growth; continued spread of the information revolution; and technological innovations, such as those with regard to disease prevention and treatment.

Global Trends and Institutional Framework

Although these external factors are too many and too complex for us to reliably predict their impact, what we can do is recall some of the most significant and broad global trends that are likely to exert a powerful influence on India's progress over the coming two decades.

1. Population Growth

Global population will continue to grow from 6 billion to around 7.5 billion people, fuelling a large increase in global demand for food, goods and services. Life expectancy will rise significantly, leading to a larger proportion of the aged in all regions. At the same time a swelling of the working age population will lead to a significant increase in the global labour force.

2. Economic Expansion

The phenomenal achievements of the last half century have been the results of a fortuitous blend of forces — the absence of a world war, the spread of democracy to countries around the globe, rising levels of education everywhere, rising social aspirations and expectations, rapid technological development and diffusion, advances in the science and the practice of management, and development of a more efficient and sophisticated economic and financial organisation for global commerce. All of these driving forces should continue to exert strong positive pressure for global economic expansion in the next century. If world real GDP continues to expand at an average rate of 3.14 per cent per annum as it did over the past 12 years, real world GDP will increase by 85 per cent over the next 20 years. A substantial rise in incomes and living standards will act as an additional stimulus to global demand for food, manufactured goods, services and energy.

3. Growth of World Trade

World trade grew by an average of about 7 per cent per annum in the decade of 1990s. By reducing and eventually eliminating all forms of trade barriers, the emerging institutional framework under WTO is likely to accelerate the expansion of world trade in the coming years. This will open greater opportunities for domestic producers while making them more vulnerable to international competition. At the same time, with the spread of new technologies and production capabilities, economies of scale are becoming increasingly important in reducing costs and prices. Increasingly, single countries or even single producers are becoming globally dominant in specific product categories. This trend has already resulted in global surpluses in categories such as steel, basic chemicals and computer memory chips. Growing surpluses will bring even greater competition between companies and countries producing the same products, as well as cheaper products for consumers, and higher standards of living. Opportunities in business will gradually shift from volume production to special value-added categories of products and services.

4. Growth of Services Sector

The driving force for economic growth and employment will

increasingly come from the services sector. Rising living standards will fuel the demand for commercial, social and community services. Construction, retailing, education, health, entertainment and tourism will expand more rapidly than ever before. The incorporation of services under the WTO framework has opened up enormous opportunities for hitherto non-tradable sectors to expand their horizons across borders. This will enhance the quality, range and affordability of services to the domestic economy and add a further stimulus to a service-led economic growth around the world. At the same time, the efforts will be needed to secure a level playing field and fairness in the trading system.

5. OECD Labour Shortages

Demographic trends in the OECD countries will create acute labour shortages, opening up unprecedented opportunities for countries that can provide skilled manpower and outsourcing services. A UN study released in March 2000 estimates that the 15-nation European Community would have to accept 150 million new immigrants over the next 25 years in order to maintain the present levels of working population. By 2013, labour force growth in the USA will be zero. The UN estimates that Japan would need to admit 600,000 immigrants annually for the next 50 years in order to maintain the size of its working population at the 1995 level. Significant labour shortages will develop in the OECD countries unless immigration policies are dramatically liberalised or large numbers of manufacturing and service jobs are shifted overseas. This trend will further accelerate the outsourcing of production of goods and services to locations where infrastructure, ease of doing business, quality, costs and availability of labour are most attractive, which will be beneficial for many labour surplus countries like India.

6. Capital Flows

The new institutional framework will promote freer flow of capital and foreign investment, both direct as well as portfolio. Capital rich nations will seek out investment destinations generating higher returns. This trend will be reinforced by rising income levels and the aging of the OECD population, which will swell the size of pension, insurance and mutual funds, resulting in a continued increase in international capital flows in search of secure and attractive returns. At the same time, large manufacturing companies will increasingly move from national to global production strategies, resulting in further shifting of production and direct investment in countries or regions in which markets exist or in which production costs are lowest.

7. Technology & Infrastructure

The TRIPS will promote even faster technological innovation. Application and diffusion of technologies in a wide range of fields across international borders will also accelerate. Agricultural technology, biotechnology, information & communications technology, computerised manufacturing technologies will transform the way human beings learn, communicate, produce, and care for their health. The most important technological breakthroughs of the coming decade are expected in areas such as precision farming, fuel cells, alternative energy, genetic engineering, portable information devices, robotics, mass customisation, and computerised health care. Application of computers will continue to spread rapidly, influencing all aspects of the global society, especially communication, manufacturing, finance and trade, scientific research, education, and medicine. The cost of global communications will continue to decline rapidly, reducing barriers of distance and making global production, distribution and marketing strategies more viable.

Implications and Options for India

1. Trade in goods

Liberalisation of trade will open up new opportunities for export of goods, while increasing pressures on India's domestic industry to cope with competition from imports, especially from China. The global market for textiles and clothing will expand dramatically and the phasing out of quantitative restrictions will increase trade in these categories. But India's ability to export will depend on its capacity to keep pace with the rising international standards of price, quality, productivity, and service. Global trade in agricultural products will also grow rapidly, though it is not yet clear to what extent the OECD countries will remove the barriers and subsidies that hinder exports to these markets. However, India's ability to become a major exporter of agricultural products will depend most on its ability to improve crop quality and productivity, while lowering costs to international levels. India missed out on the boom in manufactured exports that occurred from the 1970s to 1990s. Increasing overcapacity in basic manufacturing industries, coupled with mechanisation of processes, which eliminates the advantage of low cost labour, will limit future opportunities and benefits for export of manufactured commodity goods such as cars, TVs, and computers. Future opportunities for manufactured exports will be focused on the high end of the technology chain, computerised, customised manufacturing processes and sophisticated engineering and capital goods, areas in which India has not yet strongly positioned itself internationally.

2. Trade in services

The World Bank estimates that India will possess the fourth largest economy in the world by 2020. The emerging global scenario will open up greater opportunities for countries with a surplus of well-educated, highly skilled labour that can provide an attractive commercial environment for the outsourcing of manufacturing and service businesses from high and even middle income countries. India's recent boom in outsourcing of IT services, further facilitated by declining costs of international communication and transportation, only points to the wide range of economic opportunities existing in the manufacturing and service businesses. At the same time, the pressure for export of highly educated and highly skilled individuals will also increase, so that a significant migration of scientific, engineering and medical talent is likely to continue. Steps however need to be taken to ensure that such migration is not detrimental to the country's development.

Export of services is a field in which India can excel. Computerisation, coupled with low-cost global telecommunications are generating rapid growth of trade in service businesses, such as software and IT enabled services. This trend will further accelerate, opening up vast opportunities for countries with the capacity to deliver low-cost, high-quality services. India already commands an impressive 18.5 per cent share in the global market for customised software and the Indian software industry is the fastest growing in the world. A NASSCOM-McKinsey report estimated that by 2008, the global market for IT enabled services alone will exceed $ 1,000 billion, and that India's export of IT services will exceed $50 billion, which is double the country's total export of goods and services in 2000. In addition, India's established credentials in IT and IT enabled services can be leveraged to develop a competitive advantage in other fields, including other branches of engineering, branches of scientific research, especially biotechnology, medicine, pharmaceuticals, and agriculture, as well as education. Performance in these sectors will depend on the country's capacity to generate larger numbers of well-educated and competent scientists, engineers and professionals.

3. Capital Flows and FDI

The enlargement of the international capital market will open up increasing opportunities for India to attract foreign direct and institutional investment. Foreign direct investment (FDI) expanded globally from $159 billion in 1991 to $1,270 billion in 2000, but with an increasing proportion of these flows moving between developed nations. During this period, FDI flows to India increased six-fold to $2.3 billion, which represents less than 0.2 per cent of global FDI. The amount of capital globally available will continue to grow, but improvements in infrastructure and elimination of bureaucratic barriers will be major determinants of India's success in attracting a greater share of FDI flows. The size and prosperity of China's non-resident population has been a vital link for the channelling of technology, investment and business back to the mainland. A similar mobilisation of India's expatriate population could have momentous impact on the inflow of FDI in 2020. Likewise, multinational investments in India should be encouraged, especially in technology-intensive sectors where they can supplement and strengthen India's technological capabilities.

4. Technology

India's technology policy needs to be reformulated in the light of the emerging international economic environment, to capitalise on the accelerated global development and diffusion of technologies, and keep pace with more demanding international standards for cost, quality and productivity. India will need to be far more aggressive in acquiring and applying advanced technologies in a wide range of fields, including agriculture, information technology, energy, health and education. At the same time, India can also aspire to become an important contributor to the expansion of global frontiers of technology by building upon and leveraging its already significant achievements in fields such as pharmaceuticals, biotechnology, software, space and energy. It can also revive, simultaneously, it's traditional knowledge and technologies through formal R&D efforts.

7

Peace and Security

India is in the midst of a great experiment. It is in the process of transforming a weak agrarian economy into a modern multi-dimensional economic enterprise and a traditional stratified society into an egalitarian society, while simultaneously fashioning and transforming itself into a modern democracy through consultative politics. It is inevitable that the rapid social, economic, technological and political development of one billion people should cause turbulence. Yet it is essential that this turbulence be managed and confined within limits that preserve the social fabric and cultural values and permit the nation's transformation to continue.

Underlying all our plans and hopes for a better future, underpinning all our efforts to evolve into a harmonious and prosperous democratic nation, is the shared aspiration of all Indian people for peace. Peace is not merely the absence or avoidance of conflict. It is the essential foundation for all human and social development, the fertile ground on which we can strive to elevate our minds in knowledge, hone our productive skills, strengthen our physical infrastructure, and fashion our multitudinous communities into a strong, united and harmonious nation.

The challenges to peace are numerous and they come from all directions — from outside our border and within, as well as from within our minds. Our capacity to preserve and build lasting peace for all Indians will depend on the strength of our military to defend our borders and the potential of our economy to generate increasing employment and income opportunities for all citizens. Our education system will need to inculcate knowledge and skills in our youth. Our legal and judicial system will be required to safeguard the rights of individuals and communities. Our scientists and engineers will have to develop and harness technologies for the benefit of the people. Most of all, the wisdom and determination of our political leaders to remove injustices and to direct the collective energies of the nation for greater achievement in every field of endeavour will go a long way towards maintaining peace and harmony in the country.

Revolution of Rising Expectations

It is widely believed that poverty begets violence, but if that were true then violence both within the country and around the world would be rapidly diminishing, for both India and the world have attained unprecedented levels of development. But on closer examination it appears that violence is often associated with higher levels of development, because of the widening gap that emerges between peoples' aspirations and their accomplishments. Development leads to an awakening of human aspirations — a raising of expectations that releases people's energy and initiative for improving their lives. Yet, as it proceeds, the gap between those rising aspirations and present conditions widens. Up to a point, the widening gap acts like a voltage differential, increasing the force available for progress. But beyond that point, the widening gap leads to increasing frustration, resentment, instability and violence.

The greatest global challenge facing the international community as well as our own country is this transnational revolution of rising expectations. Recent advances in communications and information, coupled with rising levels of education, have further hastened and intensified this revolution by spreading awareness and raising aspirations. This revolution presents a challenge that must be managed by socio-economic advancement, social justice and political leadership. The peace of our nation as well as that of the world community will depend on our ability to channel the energies released by this movement into constructive initiatives for national and global prosperity.

Conventional wisdom has tended to treat national security and national defence as synonymous, but whereas defence is primarily concerned with military preparedness to combat external threats, national security covers a much broader spectrum of challenges, threats and responses. National security can be conceived of as the preservation of core values and vital interests critical to the nation-state from external and internal challenges and threats. Although we distinguish between the external and internal, in fact the two spheres are closely related. The political, economic, social and military spheres are mutually dependent.

Internal security problems in a newly emerging, independent, developing country like India essentially grow out of the laborious processes of nation-state building. At the root of the problem lies the issue of economic disparities and social inequities. Development tends to reduce the extent of these disparities in some ways while aggravating them in others. It increases the life expectancy nutritional security, health, education, social and legal protection, and economic opportunities of the masses, while at the same time enabling the more talented, enterprising, fortunate or unscrupulous to derive disproportionately greater benefits and leaving others untouched or even harmed by the general progress. Economic disparities aggravate perceptions of difference between sub-national, linguistic and communal groups, fostering ethnicity and communalism. A positive strategy for national security must reinforce the secular and democratic values of the Indian nation which derive their strength from our culture, civilization and freedom struggle.

External security depends on national power. It requires a continous enhancement of the country's capacity to use its tangible and intangible resources in such a manner as to affect the behaviour of other nations. While power is often conceived in narrow terms as military power, in the world that is emerging it must be much more broadly conceived to include political, economic, technological, social and intellectual dimensions. A vibrant economy and a leading role in international affairs may be as important as a strong military to the preservation and development of national power.

International affairs have been altered so radically by the end of the Cold War, and more recently by emergence of an international coalition against terrorism, that it is difficult to anticipate the complextion of the international environment for peace and security two decades hence. However, we can identify several of the factors that have consistently influenced our security environment in the past and which are likely to remain active for years to come.

Factors influencing Security Environment in 2020

- The twin revolutions of rising expectations and information-communications will continue.
- The fundamental ideological conflict between Pakistan and India is unlikely to be resolved without a major social-political change in Pakistan.
- Territorial disputes with neighbours that have defied resolution for fifty years may not lend themselves for easy solution.
- Religious extremism and radical politics will continue to have adverse impact on our core values.
- Rising dependence on energy imports will make us increasingly vulnerable economically, as well as diplomatically.
- Public opinion, both domestic and international, and the media will be increasingly important forces in international affairs.
- The international order is likely to evolve into a polycentric configuration with its centre of gravity shifting increasingly to Asia, which will include seven out of the ten largest economies and six out of the eight nuclear weapon states.
- The increasing economic and military strength of China may pose a serious challenge to India's security unless adequate measures are taken to fortify our own strengths.

The current global security paradigm is a competitive system founded upon the relative military power of nation states. The competitive security paradigm is a state-centered and egocentric approach in which the security of each nation is perceived in terms of its military superiority over potential adversaries. The push of each nation for unlimited security through military power is inherently de-stabilising, since it inevitably increases the level of insecurity of other sovereign states. In practice, the effort of nations to arm themselves against perceived external threats generates a sense of insecurity among other nations and compels them in turn of increase military preparedness, thus initiating a vicious spiral, as it did during the Cold War. The highly militarised approach contains an in-built mechanism for escalation that was responsible for the growth of global military expenditure to an all time peak of $1.2 trillion in 1988. The competitive security paradigm cannot provide a stable basis for global peace and security. What is needed is a quantum shift from the competitive security paradigm to a cooperative security system in which countries mutually and collectively agree to refrain from acts of aggression and to protect each other from such acts by any nation. We are now at a historic crossroads: one path leads us back to a static, unstable and exclusive competitive security paradigm; the other leads to a far more stable and dynamic cooperative security paradigm, inclusive of all nations and responsive to future needs and challenges.

Human development in all its dimensions is and will remain our highest strategic priority. Peace in search of human development must not only be durable but also seek harmony between peace and security at different levels. Internationally, we must gravitate from a state-centered, egocentric and competitive security paradigm to a co-operative security paradigm that enhances the security of each nation by reducing potential threats to all nations.

8

Governance

India's economic and technological transition is accompanied by a multifaceted political transformation which may well be slower, less clearly defined and less visible, but will nonetheless have profound impact on the functioning of the government 20 years from now. The main consequences of that transformation are likely to include:

1. Decentralisation and People's Participation

- Devolution of power to local bodies will continue at an accelerated rate. Pressure from the grassroots will increasingly supplant governance from the top down.
- Local communities will come to depend less on state and central government action and more on their own initiative and organisational capacity.
- Financial devolution will give local bodies more authority to levy taxes and greater control over the use of local natural resources. It will also make them increasingly responsible for financing local infrastructure.
- Direct democracy through gram sabhas, as opposed to representative democracy, will become more prevalent at the local level. People at the local level will be more directly involved in setting priorities for distribution of resources and managing local projects.
- A better educated and better informed electorate will be increasingly demanding of its rights and increasingly critical of non-performing governments and their individual members.

2. Efficiency, Transparency and Accountability

- Government agencies of all types at all levels will be more responsive and accountable to the public as customers.
- Mechanisms will be evolved to increase transparency and reduce corruption.
- E-government will improve responsiveness and reduce corruption in some areas. Computerisation of information systems coupled with downsizing, higher recruitment standards and stricter discipline will increase administrative efficiency.
- The educational, technical and professional qualifications of political leaders will rise.

The problems of governance 20 years from now will still include those issues which occupy our attention today — transparency, corruption, non-responsiveness, favouritism, bureaucracy, inefficiency, lack of accountability, ineffectiveness of implementation, etc. But rising expectations, increasing levels of education, greater access to information and greater prosperity will be working to mitigate these factors to a large extent.

Worldwide E-governance is such a recent development, that it is difficult to assess its potential impact 20 years hence. However, the plans and projects already being implemented by various state governments within the country suggest that it has the potential, if fully harnessed and rightly utilised, to radically improve the speed, convenience, quality and transparency of public administrative services, while enhancing the ability of individual citizens to express and exercise their democratic rights.

The essence of good governance is the capacity to envision the opportunities that lead to a better future, to build a broad consensus in support of that vision, to take the bold decisions necessary to realise the vision, and to exercise the determination and perseverance required for overcoming obstacles and resistances that arise along the way.

9

Conclusion

Best-case Scenario for India 2020

Identifying potentials and anticipating the challenges to our future progress in different sectors of the national economy does not constitute a vision of the country's future. These disparate threads need to be woven together to reflect the integrated nature of our national life. Then, there still remains the question of whether to be preoccupied by the negative possibilities or to throw our full weight behind efforts to fully realise the positive potentials revealed by this analysis. That will determine whether we regard the following statement as a promising glimpse of what India can become in 2020, or as mere fantasy and wishful thinking.

India 2020 will be bustling with energy, entrepreneurship and innovation. The country's 1.35 billion people will be better fed, dressed and housed, taller and healthier, more educated and longer living than any generation in the country's long history. Illiteracy and all major contagious diseases will have disappeared. School enrolment from age 6 to 14 will near 100 per cent and drop out rates will fall to less than one in twenty.

A second productivity revolution in Indian agriculture, coupled with diversification to commercial crops, agri-business, processing industries, agro-exports and massive efforts towards afforestation and wasteland development will generate abundant farm and non-farm employment opportunities for the rural workforce. These in turn will stimulate demand for consumer goods and services, giving a fillip to the urban economy and the informal sector as well as rapid expansion of the services sector.

India's claim to the title Silicon Valley of Asia will be followed by the diversification from IT to biotechnology, medical sciences and other emerging fields of technology, widening the field of India's international competitiveness and generating a large number of employment opportunities for the educated youth. These developments, driven by the firm commitment of the government and a quantum expansion of vocational training programmes, will ensure jobs for all by 2020.

Inequalities between different age groups, the sexes, income groups, communities and regions will come down dramatically. The old disparities between the very rich and the poor will not have disappeared, but the nature of poverty in 2020 will not be nearly as harsh and oppressive as it was at the turn of the millennium. Regional disparities will remain visible, though all regions will have advanced significantly in two decades. India's achievements have been fuelled by the realisation that the progress of the whole ultimately depends on the progress of its weakest links; India 2020 must be one in which all levels and sections of the population and all parts of the country march forward together towards a more secure and prosperous future.

The increasingly congested urban traffic will be motorised as never before. Two wheelers will be ubiquitous and cars will be considered essential for most middle class families. City roads and rural highways will improve substantially in number, capacity and quality, but a four-fold multiplication in the number of vehicle will tax the urban infrastructure to the limit. Urban congestion will accelerate the movement of business, middle class families and even government offices into new self-contained suburban centres. Cell phones, computers and the Internet will permeate every aspect of life and every corner of the country.

Computerisation of education will dramatically improve the quality of instruction and the pace of learning, so that many students will complete the first twelve years of school curriculum in as little as eight. Computerised distance education will catch on in a big way and enable tens of thousands more students to opt for affordable higher education. Computerisation in government will streamline procedures and response times to a degree unimaginable now. Perceptive observers will find that India is leapfrogging directly into a predominantly service economy.

Environmental issues will remain a serious concern. Urban air pollution will come under control by strict enforcement of motor vehicle emission standards and widespread use of ethanol-blended motor fuels, but water shortages in major metropolitan areas will continue despite a national programme to popularise water harvesting techniques in both urban and rural areas. A massive afforestation programme will reverse the depletion of forest areas, raise the nation's Green cover to 33 per cent of area, generate millions of rural employment opportunities, and provide abundant renewable energy from biomass power production.

India will be much more integrated with the global economy and will be a major player in terms of trade, technology and investment.

Rising levels of education, employment and income will help stabilise India's internal security and social environment. A united, and prosperous India will be far less vulnerable to external security threats.

A more prosperous India in 2020 will be characterised by a better-educated electorate and more transparent, accountable, efficient and decentralised government.

Some may regard this vision as an anxious attempt to imitate and catch up with the West. But there is an important distinction to be made between blind imitation and intelligent emulation that draws upon the discoveries and experiences of others to address universal needs common to all human beings and all societies. India, with its rich cultural heritage and thousands of years of history of civilisation, need not aspire to become like country A or B. For India, realising the vision for 2020 is not an end in itself, but rather an essential condition for allowing the spirit of this country to emerge and flourish.

Decision Points

There is a natural temptation to attempt to reduce two decades of future progress to a concise formula and prepare a manifesto of policies or strategies that will enable the country to realise its full potential during that period. But a list of such policies or strategies will always remain unsatisfactory unless it is made comprehensive, and a comprehensive list needs to include hundreds of necessary and desirable initiatives.

However, in addition to these policy and strategy prescriptions, or rather underlying and supporting them, there are some nodal points of action which, when touched, can release the enormous pent-up energy of the society and throw it into constructive action. It is well that we conclude our summary by identifying those nodal points which will be most powerful for propelling forward the development of Indian society over the next two decades.

These nine nodes are not independent powers. Each draws upon and contributes to the power of the other seven. They are mutually supportive and reinforcing. They are not a hierarchy of powers that can be developed sequentially, but rather eight essential forces that need to be developed simultaneously. As peace and education are essential for growth of employment and living standards, so are food security and employment opportunities essential for peace and social stability, and so forth.

But beyond these physical, social and mental powers, this country possesses something even more powerful and essential to its existence. India is a nation with a soul and a great spiritual tradition founded upon faith in the power of the spirit to create and manifest in the world. It is our spiritual values, our psychic essence, which is the core strength of Indian civilisation that has sustained it for millenniums and will elevate the quality of our national life in future. These values possess the ultimate power both for national prosperity and to propel India to be a proud member of the world community. *True spirituality will not make us less tolerant.* Though our spiritual tradition takes on an infinite variety of forms, they all share a common faith in our capacity as human beings to realise whatever we aspire for.

Our future depends not on what will happen to us, but on what we decide to become, and on the will to create it.

Nodal Points of Indian Prosperity

1. *Peace, Security and National Unity* — Physical security both from external and internal threats — strong national defence, domestic law enforcement and social harmony.
2. *Food & Nutritional Security* — A vibrant, highly productive commercial farm sector that can ensure food & nutritional security, generate employment opportunities, stimulate industrialisation, and produce renewable energy from biomass and fuel crops.
3. *Jobs for All* — A constitutional commitment to ensure the right of all citizens to a sustainable livelihood that will provide them with the purchasing power needed to freely cast their economic votes in the market place.
4. *Knowledge* — 100 per cent literacy & school education, and vocational training for all new entrants to the workforce, to equip youth with the knowledge and skills needed to thrive in an increasingly competitive world: adult education programmes to compensate working age school drop-outs for the lack of education, and continued investment in science and technology to improve productivity, quality of life and the environment.
5. *Health* — Expansion of the infrastructure for public health and medical care to ensure health for all.
6. *Technology & Infrastructure* — Continuous expansion of the physical infrastructure for rapid low-cost transportation and communication that is required for rapid economic growth and international competitiveness. Application of computers to improve access to knowledge and information, and increase in the speed, efficiency and convenience of activities in all fields of life.
7. *Globalisation* — Successful integration of India with world economy.
8. *Good Governance* — Farsighted and dynamic leadership to maximise national prosperity, individual freedom and social equity through responsive, transparent and accountable administration that removes all the bottlenecks to economic development.
9. *Work Values* — Activation of all these nodal points requires firm and determined adherence to high values, including prompt decision-making, disciplined execution, systematic implementation, finely tuned co-ordination, unceasing effort and endurance.

Annexures

Annexure 1

Rabindranath Tagore's Vision

> *Where the mind is without fear and the head is held high.*
> *Where knowledge is free.*
> *Where the world has not been broken up into fragments*
> *By narrow domestic walls.*
> *Where words come out from the depth of truth.*
> *Where tireless striving stretches its arms towards perfection.*
> *Where the clear stream of reason has not lost its way*
> *Into the dreary desert sand of dead habit.*
> *Where the mind is led forward by Thee*
> *Into ever-widening thought and action.*
> *Into that heaven of freedom, my Father, let my country awake.*
>
> *Rabindranath Tagore*

The vision articulated by Rabindranath Tagore is all encompassing in every sense. It has laid down what he considered to be the basic constituents of the "heaven of freedom". We can identify eight components of this vision reflected in the poem quoted earlier, which we can attempt to translate into operational terms for India's vision 2020.

Where the mind is without fear — Peace and security, internal as well as external, is the first and most essential foundation for the nation's future progress. Fearlessness can only be attained when this security extends to cover, over and above our physical safety, our social rights and economic well being, to eliminate all forms of vulnerability and discrimination.

Where the head is held high — Self-respect and self-esteem are the psychological foundations for the development of individuality and individual initiative, which are the means through which the nation builds its strength and fulfils its aspirations. The nation prospers through the development and flowering of all its citizens as individuals. Health, education and employment opportunities for all, and awareness of our rich spiritual and cultural heritage are the essential bases for fostering self-respect and self-esteem.

Where knowledge is free — Development takes place when people become aware of opportunities for advancement and acquire the knowledge needed to convert those opportunities into practical accomplishments. Knowledge in the form of education, technology and access to a wide range of information is a catalyst for individual and social progress. The free flow of knowledge is the basis for a free and prosperous society.

Where the world has not been broken up into fragments by narrow domestic walls — The spirit of globalisation which is rapidly reshaping the world today cannot be better expressed. The accelerated flow and exchange of trade, capital, technology, information and people will create unprecedented opportunities for the progress and prosperity of all countries that can transcend the narrow confines of national boundaries. India can however realise its full potential in the wider world only when it is internally united, surmounting all the centrifugal forces that overlook our common heritage and accentuate our differences.

Where words come out from the depth of truth — Integrity, honesty and trustworthiness are the essential foundations for a successful democracy and a prosperous society. Both good governance and commercial success demand rigorous standards of transparency, accountability and reliability in word and action.

Where tireless striving stretches its arms towards perfection — Prosperity is the result of productivity and efficiency which require the highest level of productive skills, technological excellence and human effort.

Where the clear stream of reason has not lost its way into the dreary desert sand of dead habit — Nations develop by choosing the best the future has to offer, while being willing to discard outmoded ideas and behaviours that retard future progress and even threaten to undermine the country's unity and strength.

Where the mind is led forward by Thee into ever-widening thought and action — Education, innovation and creativity are the ultimate driving forces for the continous advancement of scientific knowledge and material accomplishment.

These threads from Rabindranath's poem are the vital strands from which a fulfilling vision of India 2020 can be woven.

Annexure II

No.M-110022/1/2000-PP
Government of India
Planning Commission

Yojana Bhavan, Sansad Marg,

New Delhi, the 12th May 2000

ORDER

It has been decided to set up a Committee on Vision 2020 for India. The composition of the Committee will be as follows.

Chairman

Dr. S.P. Gupta, Member, Planning Commission, New Delhi.

Member

1. Dr. R.K. Pachauri, Director, Tata Energy Research Institute, New Delhi.
2. Dr. R. Radhakrishna, Vice Chancellor, Andhra University, Vishakhapatnam.
3. Dr. Panjab Singh, Director, Indian Agriculture Research Institute, New Delhi.
4. Prof. Ashish Bose, Former Professor, Institute of Economic Growth, Delhi.
5. Prof. Pravin Visaria, Director, Institute of Economic Growth, Delhi.
6. Shri K.L. Thapar, Director, Asian Institute of Transport Development, New Delhi.
7. Dr. Padam Singh, Additional Director General, ICMR, New Delhi.
8. Prof. C.P. Ramaswamy, Centre for Policy Research, New Delhi.
9. Shri K.C. Sivaramakrishnan, Centre for Policy Research, New Delhi.

10. Dr. V.A. Pai Panandiker, Director, Centre for Policy Research, New Delhi.

11. Shri Jasjit Singh, Director, Indian Institute of Defence Studies and Analysis, New Delhi.

12. Prof. V.R. Panchmukhi, Director-General, Research and Information System for the Non-Aligned and other Developing Countries, New Delhi.

13. Prof. P.V. Indiresan, Centre for Policy Research, New Delhi.

14. Dr. J.S. Rajput, Director, NCERT, New Delhi.

15. Dr. Prema Ramachandran, Adviser (Health), Planning Commission, New Delhi.

16. Dr. Pronab Sen, Adviser (PP), Planning Commission, New Delhi.

17. Dr. Shovan Ray, Consultant, Planning Commission, New Delhi.

2. The Committee will be serviced by the Perspective Planning Division with Shri J.N. Maggo, Joint Adviser, (IIP) acting as Secretary to the Committee.

3. The Committee may co-opt other experts as and when deemed necessary.

4. Non-officials shall be entitled to TA/DA as permissible to Grade I officers of Government of India and the expenditure will be borne by Planning Commission. The TA/DA of Government and Public Sector officials will be borne by their respective organisations.

(Arvind K. Alipura)

Director (Admn.)

Members Co-opted Subsequently

1. Dr. Amit S. Ray, Consultant, Planning Commission, New Delhi. (Member Secretary, Vision 2020 Committee)
2. Dr. Garry Jacobs, Mother Service Society, Plot No. 4, Venkata Nagar, Pondicherry-605011.
3. Dr. K. Srinivasan, Population Foundation of India, B-28, Qutab Institutional Area, Tara Crescent, New Delhi-110016.
4. Shri R. Srinivasan, B-4, Hiranya Apartments, (off Greenway Road), Mylapore, Chennai-600028.
5. Shri G.N. Kathpalia, E-190, Greater Kailash, Delhi-110048
6. Shri P. Chaturvedi, Chairman, The Instt. of Engineering, Engineer Bhavan, Bahadur Shah Zafar Marg, New Delhi-110001.
7. Prof. Amitabh Kundu, CSRD, School of Social Sciences, JNU, New Delhi.
8. Dr. Krishna Sondhi, 7, Amrita Shergill Marg, New Delhi-110003.
9. Prof. Ramaswamy R. Iyer, Centre for Policy Research, Dharma Marg, Chanakya Puri, New Delhi-110021.
10. Shri Anwar ul-Hoda, ICRIER, India Habitat Centre, Lodhi Road, New Delhi.
11. Dr. Nagesh Kumar, RIS, Zone IV B 4th Floor, India Habitat Centre, Lodhi Road, New Delhi-110003.
12. Dr. Sarala Gopalan, 138 Vasant Enclave, New Delhi-110057.
13. Dr. Hira Singh, 183, Munirka Enclave, New Delhi-110067.
14. Shri M.C. Verma, Adviser, Ministry of Labour, 1st Floor, Shram Shakti Bhavan, New Delhi-110001.
15. Shri M.C. Gupta, Director, Indian Instt. of Public Administration, Indraprastha Estate, Ring Road, New Delhi-110022.
16. Shri H.S. Saksena, Editor, Eastern Anthropologist, Lucknow.
17. Dr. Manas Bhattacharya, Dy. Director General, Dept. of

Telecommunications, Ministry of Telecom & IT, Govt. of India.

18. Shri Mahesh Kapoor, New Delhi.
19. Shri H. Ramachandran, Director, IAMR, New Delhi.
20. Major Gen. S.S. Sandhu, New Delhi.
21. Shri Durganand Jha, Executive Director, Association for Social and Economic Transformation.

The Terms of Reference of this Committee are:

1. To prepare an outlook for India in 2020, especially focusing on the opportunities and challenges.
2. To envision the possibilities of India's development potential over the next two decades in a multi dimensional framework, including aspects of human development, social & physical infrastructure, knowledge resources & technology, energy & environment, economy, governance and security.
3. To seek inputs from members of the Committee and from other sources from within and outside the Planning Commission.
4. To come out with a document on "India: Vision 2020".

LIST OF CONTRIBUTORS

1. Dr. Manas Bhattacharya: Telecom
2. Mr. P. Chaturvedi: Energy
3. Dr. Sarala Gopalan: Empowerment of Women
4. Mr. M.C. Gupta: Governance (published)
5. Mr. Anwar-ul-Hoda: International Economy
6. Dr. P.V. Indiresan: Rural Development
7. Prof. Ramaswamy R. Iyer: Water (published)
8. Mr. G. Jacobs: Knowledge Society
9. Prof. Amitabh Kundu: Urbanisation
10. Mr. G.N. Kathpalia: Water
11. Mr. Mahesh Kapoor: Transport
12. Dr. Nagesh Kumar: External Sector
13. Mr. R.K. Pachauri: Energy, Environment
14. Dr. J.S. Rajput: Education
15. Dr. H. Ramachandran: Governance
16. Dr. R. Radhakrishna: Food Security, Nutrition and Poverty
17. Mr. H.S. Saksena: Vulnerable Groups
18. Maj-Gen. S.S. Sandhu: Older Persons
19. Dr. S.K. Sarkar: Energy
20. Dr. Rohit Sarkar: Financial Sector
21. Dr. Hira Singh: Social Defence
22. Air Comdr. Jasjit Singh: Peace
23. Dr. Padam Singh: Fertility, Mortality
24. Dr. Panjab Singh: Agriculture
25. Dr. K. Srinivasan: Population
26. Mr. R. Srinivasan: Health
27. Dr. Krishan Sondhi: Information Technology
28. Swami Agnivesh: Child Labour
29. Mr. M.C. Verma: Social Dimension

From Planning Commission:

30. LEM Division: Employment
31. Health Division (Dr. Prema Ramachandran): Health Nutrition, Population

Andhra Pradesh

Vision : 2020

Andhra Pradesh: Vision 2020

"Our vision of Andhra Pradesh is a state where poverty is totally eradicated; where every man, woman and child has access to not just the basic minimum needs, but to all the opportunities to lead a happy and fulfilling life; a knowledge and learning society built on the values of hard work, honesty, discipline and a collective sense of purpose."

— *N. Chandrababu Naidu*

Andhra Pradesh has set itself an ambitious vision. By 2020, the State will have achieved a level of development that will provide its people tremendous opportunities to achieve prosperity and wellbeing and enjoy a high quality of life.

To attain this level of development, the State will have to embark on a vigorous effort to create economic growth. Development, particularly social development, will require the creation of economic opportunity, mainly through the growth of the economy. Economic opportunity can be created even in the most adverse circumstances. Japan and Germany created great opportunities in the post-war era by developing excellence in manufacturing. Singapore, with minimal natural resources, raised the standard of living of its people by creating a free port and a trading hub in its island nation. In the same way, through innovation and resourcefulness, Andhra Pradesh will have to stimulate the growth of the three major sectors of its economy: agriculture, industry, and services.

Economic growth will stimulate development in two ways. First, it will increase incomes for the people by creating employment opportunities. Second, it will generate additional resources for the Government. The Government will invest these resources mainly in social development, that is, eradicating poverty, improving education and health, promoting rural and urban development, and providing services such as housing, water, power, transportation, and so on.

Of course, this can be achieved only with the active participation of the people in the development of the State. The Government, therefore, looks to the people to become its partners in progress, striving together to achieve the level of development that Vision 2020 stands for.

What will life in the State be like if this level of social development and economic growth is achieved?

By 2020, every individual in Andhra Pradesh will be able to lead a comfortable life, filled with opportunities to learn, develop skills, and earn a livelihood. Poverty will have been eradicated and current inequalities will have disappeared. Disadvantaged groups — scheduled castes, scheduled tribes, backward classes, and minorities — as well as other groups in need of special attention, such as women and children, will be empowered and provided with the opportunities they need to achieve their full potential. The genuinely vulnerable — the old, the infirm, and the disabled — will be able to lead a secure and dignified life. Every child in the State will be well fed, healthy and will go to school and learn. A girl child born in this year will have as many chances as her brothers will to go to school, find a job and live a healthy and productive life.

No family will lack basic needs like food, clothing and shelter. Every family will be able to live in hygienic surroundings, and enjoy the benefits of clean air and water. Power will be available to run appliances, radios and televisions; transport will be at hand to go to work or seek entertainment and so will telephones to get important jobs done or simply keep in touch with relatives and friends. Families will continue to promote social values, encourage hard work, and continually strive for a better life.

Andhra Pradesh will have a skilled workforce that stands for quality, productivity, workmanship and initiative; and policies and procedures that make it easy to do business in the State.

Agriculture, industry and services businesses will have power, transport, telecommunications, in fact, all the infrastructure they require to grow strongly and profitably. This will make investors favour Andhra Pradesh in their investment decisions.

Andhra Pradesh's people will be able to look forward to exciting opportunities in a flourishing economy with thriving agriculture, industry and services sectors. If they live in rural areas, they will earn profitable livelihoods from a revitalised agriculture sector, find jobs on poultry farms, food processing or fisheries units, or be able to set up their own small-scale enterprises.

If they live in Andhra Pradesh's cities, they will be able to work in exports firms, garments manufacturing enterprises, construction and real estate companies, travel agencies, tourism offices, and software development firms, among many others. In both villages and cities, they will be able to set up retail outlets, restaurants, and other such services. To equip them to be successful in their jobs and businesses, they will have access to knowledge and training through vocational education and skill-building institutions and the benefits of technology transfer and small technologies.

Everyone will benefit from a government that is truly 'for the people', which enables individuals and businesses to achieve their full potential, and is transparent and efficient in its functioning. In short, Andhra Pradesh will be a vibrant and prosperous place, a State that sets the standards for a high quality life.

To achieve this vision, Andhra Pradesh has set itself the following mission (Exhibit 1):

- Eradicate poverty and take care of its old, infirm, and genuinely needy.
- Enable its people to learn, earn, and lead healthful and productive lives.
- Promote small families for a healthy and wealthy society.
- Give its children a happy childhood and every opportunity to achieve their full potential.
- Empower and support its women and girls to fulfil their roles as equal shapers with men of the economy and society.
- Create the resources its people will need, such as capital

and infrastructure, to transform their own futures.

- Enable its farmers, entrepreneurs, and professionals to make agriculture flourish and build thriving industries and services businesses.
- Embrace innovation and the latest know-how to grow its crops, make its goods, and provide high quality services.
- Safeguard its environment and make its villages and cities clean, green and safe to live in.
- Make its government simple, transparent, accountable and responsive.
- Ensure that its people continue to have a strong voice and role in the governance of their State.

Exhibit 1

Andhra Pradesh's Mission

- Eradicate poverty and take care of its old, infirm, and genuinely needy
- Enable its people to learn, earn, and lead healthful and productive lives
- Promote small families for a healthy and wealthy society
- Give its children a happy childhood and every opportunity to achieve their full potential
- Empower and support its women and girls to fulfil their roles as equal shapers with men of the economy and society
- Create the resources its people will need, such as capital and infrastructure, to transform their own futures
- Enable its farmers, entrepreneurs, and professionals to make agriculture flourish and build thriving industries and services businesses
- Embrace innovation and the latest know-how to grow its crops, make its good, and provide high quality services
- Safeguard its environment and make its cities and villages clean, green and safe to live in
- Make its government simple, transparent, accountable and responsive
- Ensure that its people continue to have a strong voice and role in the governance of their state

> The average per capita income will need to increase nine times, with incomes for the poor growing much more rapidly.

This is an exciting and ambitious vision and a challenging mission to realise. What does Andhra Pradesh need to do to achieve these goals?

Andhra Pradesh's economy will have to be stimulated to grow by 9-10 per cent a year, on an average, in real terms for the next 25 years. The average per capita income will need to increase nine times, with incomes for the poor growing much more rapidly. Population growth will have to be contained at less than 1 per cent (0.8 per cent) a year and at least 18-20 million new jobs will have to be created (Exhibit 2).

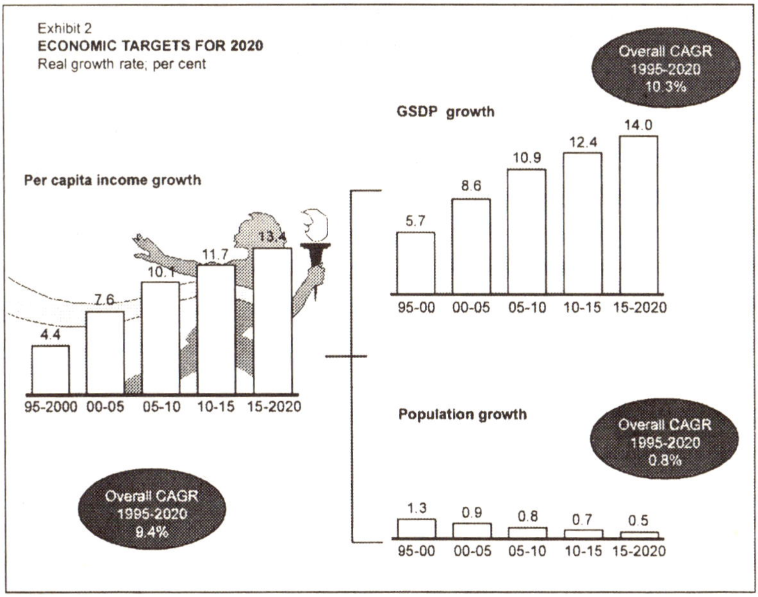

Each major sector of the economy – agriculture, industry, and services – will have to grow strongly. Agriculture will have to quadruple in size and grow at an average rate of 6 per cent a year (in real terms), making Andhra Pradesh a powerhouse in Indian agriculture. Industry will have to grow to 13 times its current size and achieve an annual growth of 11 per cent. The services sector will need to expand to almost 16 times its current size and grow at the rate of 12 per cent a year (Exhibit 3). Comprising more than 60 per cent of the economy by 2020, this sector will have to be the major generator of new jobs, especially in rural areas. Overall, while agriculture will continue to grow strongly, the economy will undergo a transformation from a predominantly agrarian to an industry- and services-led economy (Exhibit 4).

Exhibit 3
SECTORAL GROWTH TARGETS FOR 2020
Real growth rate; per cent

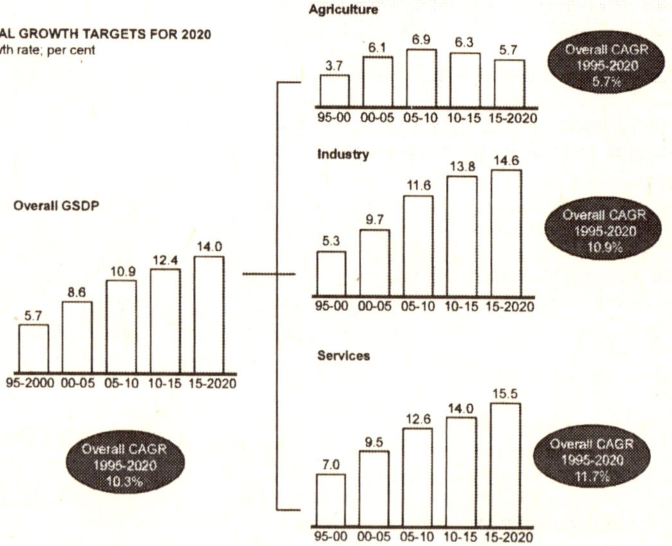

The targeted growth rates are not unprecedented. Several countries have accomplished growth in this range before. For example, China and Korea have averaged around 9 per cent growth (8.9 and 8.7 per cent respectively) for two decades (till the mid-1990s). With regard to sectoral growth, China achieved an average annual growth rate of 5.9 per cent for its agriculture sector for a ten-year period (1980-90). Over the same period, Chile's agriculture sector grew at the annual rate of 5.6 per cent. In terms of industrial growth, between 1980 and 1990, Korea achieved an annual growth rate of 13.1 per cent while China recorded 11.1 per cent. In the same decade, China's services sector grew at the rapid rate of 13.6 per cent.

Exhibit 4
CHANGE IN STRUCTURE OF THE ECONOMY IN 2020
Per cent; constant 1995-96 prices; Rs. crore

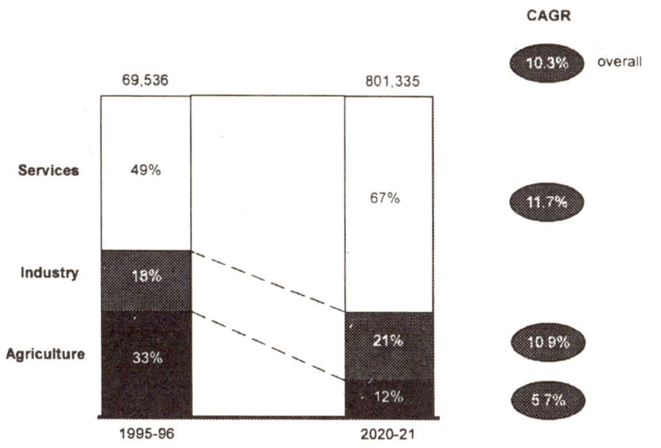

To achieve the growth levels targeted, the Government will have to seek transformation on many dimensions: at least Rs.16,00,000[1] crore will have to be invested in building infrastructure in the State[2]. The productivity of Andhra Pradesh's people will need to be rapidly increased through investments in education and health. The State is committed to achieving total literacy by 2010 and, by 2020, infant and child mortality rates of 10 per 1,000 (live births) and 20 per 1,000 respectively, and life expectancy of 68.1 years for men and 70.6 years for women.

This social and economic development will have to be buttressed by making justice available to all and maintaining law and order. The State will address itself even more vigorously to promoting peace and safety in Andhra Pradesh by controlling crime, extremism, factionalism, and communalism. Efforts will be made to remove the belief that speedy justice is unavailable to the common man and the police will be made more accountable and people-friendly.

Finally, to promote rapid development, the State Government will need to transform itself and quickly adopt a new role: from being primarily a controller of the economy, it must become a facilitator and catalyst of its growth.

How will Andhra Pradesh be able to do all this? Today, global forces are creating unprecedented opportunities for growth. Many growth opportunities have also emerged from India's ongoing economic reforms. Andhra Pradesh is in a good position to capture these opportunities – and has already made some breakthroughs in doing so. Going forward, the State can capitalise on its many strengths to create strong and rapid growth.

• *Global forces are throwing open new avenues to growth:* The world economy is becoming increasingly integrated. Realising that significant economic growth can now come from participating in world markets, nations are increasingly opening up their economies and doing away with barriers — trade, regulation, and other – which hamper the flow of investment or goods between markets. Companies are constantly looking for new markets in which to sell

1 At constant 1995-96 prices.

2 At least Rs.4,00,000 crore will have to be invested in the next 10 years to achieve the growth levels targeted.

their products and new regions in which to locate their businesses so that they become more and more competitive. Investors are searching the world for profitable investments, providing capital to anyone who has the best returns to offer. Tremendous advances in knowledge and information technology are driving this process even faster: companies (and governments) can now make quantum leaps in productivity and efficiency, leapfrogging several stages of development their predecessors had to undergo.

> The State Government will need to transform itself and quickly adopt a new role: from being primarily a controller of the economy, it must become a facilitator and catalyst of its growth.

• *India is opening its doors to growth*: Realising that it too can make this quantum leap, India has started its transition into an international, market-based economy: it has initiated the opening of its economy to foreign investors and, to some extent, its markets to the products of foreign companies. It is gradually removing barriers to trade and industry. Along with these changes in the economic sphere have come changes in the political one: power is increasingly devolving from the Centre to the states, allowing India's states to become more self-reliant in the true spirit of federalism.

• *Andhra Pradesh has achieved some breakthroughs*: In its quest to achieve strong economic growth, Andhra Pradesh has already made some significant advances. The State has attracted private investment in infrastructure; for instance, two private power plants, India's first fast-track IPP (Independent Power Producer) projects, are coming up at Jegurupadu and Kakinada. The State is increasing its attractiveness to investors by simplifying procedures (for example, establishing the State Investment Promotion Board to hasten the approval of investment proposals). And it is fast building a reputation as a key Information Technology centre in India. Finally, Andhra Pradesh has initiated pioneering programmes such as Water Users' Associations, Electronic Government, and Janmabhoomi, to ensure participatory governance and transparency, improve services, and simplify procedures.

• *Andhra Pradesh has many strengths to build on*: Andhra Pradesh has many advantages it can build on to realise its growth aspirations. The State ranks among the top five Indian states in terms of cultivable land. It has ample water resources: 60 per cent of Andhra Pradesh has ample rainfall and two major rivers of the country, the Krishna and the Godavari, flow through the State. It has the second largest mineral reserves in the country: massive deposits of coal, limestone and bauxite are to be found here.

> Andhra Pradesh has many advantages it can build on to realise its growth aspirations.

Andhra Pradesh is also strategically located. It has the second longest coastline in the country, providing several gateways for international trade. For instance, its ports provide quick access to countries such as Singapore and Malaysia. Moreover, located more or less in the centre of India, it is within easy reach of key Indian cities — Delhi, Mumbai, Calcutta, Bangalore and Chennai. The State also has emerging economic centres of national importance in Hyderabad and Visakhapatnam, the two fastest growing cities in the country. Furthermore, Andhra Pradesh has a great deal of agricultural wealth. It leads all other states in the production of poultry and is among India's top producers of fruits and rice. In addition, the State is rapidly building a reputation with Indian and international investors, especially in knowledge-based sectors such as Information Technology.

To these strengths, Andhra Pradesh will add speedy reform and capability building, giving it a significant competitive edge. Most Indian states and many other countries are anticipating opportunities and moving to capture them. What will separate the winners from the losers will be the ability to move fast, reform government, create infrastructure and develop human resources. Andhra Pradesh will move quickly on all these fronts to ensure that it emerges a winner.

The challenge ahead is to put all these opportunities and advantages to work to achieve Andhra Pradesh's Vision 2020. In other words, Andhra Pradesh needs a new and comprehensive growth agenda.

What could this growth agenda be? To achieve the level of development it has targeted, Andhra Pradesh will need a three-fold approach: (1) building capabilities, i.e., developing human resources, improving the quality of life in the State, and attracting investment in its economy; (2) focusing on high-potential sectors as its engines of growth; and (3) transforming governance, i.e., channelling the Government's efforts into enabling and facilitating economic growth (Exhibit 5). Finally, the State will have to take bold and innovative steps to finance the implementation of the vision.

Exhibit 5

The Growth Agenda for Andhra Pradesh

	Andhra Pradesh in 2020		
	Best people	*Best place to live*	*Best place to invest*
Building the capabilities of the State's people and improving the quality of life	* Skilled, productive, healthy people * Safety net for vulnerable sections of society	* Sustainable environment * Clean/liveable cities/villages * Efficient rural/ urban civic services	* Adequate and good quality infrastructure * Favourable policy and procedural environment
	Agriculture	*Industry*	*Services*
Focusing on primary "growth engines"/ important sectors	* Poultry, * Dairy * Horticulture * Rice * Fisheries * Agro-industry	* Construction * Mining * Pharmaceuticals * Small-scale industries * Labour-intensive export oriented industries (garments/leather products) * Infrastructure	* IT * Tourism * Small-scale services * Logistics * Knowledge-based services * Education * Healthcare
Transforming Government to play a facilitating role in economic development	Clean, Capable and Transparent Government that facilitates, not controls, economic development		

This growth agenda is not an ill-founded aspiration. Rather, it is based on a realistic assessment of the problems and opportunities before the State as well as its achievements. The rest of this chapter lays out the current scenario in the State, as well as the strategies for each of the three elements of the growth agenda. It also explains how the resources required for achieving the vision will be raised.

SCENARIO: PAST AND PRESENT

Despite its best endeavours, Andhra Pradesh is yet to realise its potential in terms of both social and economic development.

More than half the State's population is illiterate today. Andhra Pradesh ranks 26th out of 32 States/Union territories in the country in terms of overall literacy and 29th in literacy for Scheduled Castes and Scheduled Tribes. Though health in Andhra Pradesh has improved significantly, the State still lags behind many Indian states on key health indicators. Urban infrastructure and services are largely inadequate leading to a poor quality of life. Furthermore, despite economic growth and increasing urbanisation, the rural population has limited opportunity to productively participate in the economy. As a result, inequities between disadvantaged groups and the rest of the population have not diminished, some areas of the State have remained backward in terms of development, and poverty remains a key issue for the State.

With regard to the economy, the State's overall growth rate has been 4.6 per cent a year till recently, lower than the country's average of 5.2 per cent a year and that of India's six fastest growing states (5.7 per cent). All three sectors of Andhra Pradesh's economy, agriculture, industry, and services, have recorded slower growth than the all-India average. Agricultural growth has been affected by an underdeveloped agricultural value chain and regulation that hampers productivity. Industrial growth has been hindered by poor infrastructure, a lack of skilled labour and complex regulation. Growth in the services sector has been affected by a limited government focus on services, a lack of private investment, inadequate education facilities, and underdeveloped infrastructure.

On the fiscal front, Andhra Pradesh experienced a severe crisis from the mid-80s onwards due mainly to declining revenues and rising public expenditure on subsidies, salaries, and welfare programmes. Currently, the State is running a fiscal deficit of 3.4 per cent of GSDP. Revenues have remained low for a variety of reasons, both legislative and administrative.

Against this bleak picture, however, must be set the various steps the Government has taken to restore the health of its economy. These include a concerted effort to build human capital, augment infrastructure, improve its finances, attract investment in focus areas of the economy, and decentralise governance.

The State has increased allocations for education and health, and embarked on a programme to achieve universal primary education and strengthen primary healthcare. It has also introduced more sharply focused social welfare schemes, with an emphasis on poverty eradication and skill building for weaker sections.

In addition, the Government has acted to augment infrastructure in critical areas such as power and irrigation. In power, it has implemented a short-term programme to create additional capacity of about 2,000 MW mainly through private investment and a medium-term investment programme to create about 6,500 MW of power. In irrigation, the Government has stepped up investment in canal irrigation and encouraged private groundwater irrigation.

The State Government has also taken several steps to improve its finances. These include rationalising subsidies, reforming the tax structure, undertaking power sector reforms, and inviting private sector participation in the infrastructure sector. Perhaps, the most visible success of the Government's effort to revive the economy is the aggressive policy and action to promote investment in focus areas. The emergence of the State as a major destination for investment in Information Technology is a case in point.

The State has increased allocations for education and health, and embarked on a programme to achieve universal primary education and strengthen primary healthcare.

Another change in its approach lies in involving the people in governance. The State is committed to the devolution of power through the implementation of the 73rd and 74th Constitutional Amendments. Furthermore, to ensure participatory governance and transparency and improve services, the State has instituted the

Janmabhoomi initiative and is promoting self-help groups such as Water Users' Associations (WUAs) and School Education Committees.

The Janmabhoomi initiative closely involves the people in the choice as well as execution of development works of a defined nature and value. These works are undertaken by the people themselves without any intermediaries. To operationalise this concept, the Government has delegated the technical and administrative powers to sanction works, simplified procedures and ensured transparency in the estimates of works undertaken, including a social audit of works completed.

Self-help groups are encouraged to work with the Government to identify and solve the problems they face. Thus, through the WUAs, farmers now collectively determine the optimal distribution and use of water among themselves. Similar successes have been achieved through many other self-help groups such as Development of Women and Children in Rural Areas and Chief Minister's Empowerment of Youth.

These initiatives on many fronts have set the stage for the quantum leap Andhra Pradesh is seeking: equitable social development and rapid economic growth. To achieve these twin objectives, the State will marshal all its efforts and every resource available behind its growth agenda. The rest of this chapter lays out the strategies for each element of the growth agenda: building capabilities, focusing on high potential sectors of the economy, and transforming governance.

BUILDING CAPABILITIES

To build the capabilities of its people, the State will have to empower them so that they can act as catalysts of development. Furthermore, to achieve its ambitious targets for social justice and growth, Andhra Pradesh will have to develop its human resources, i.e., ensure that its people are educated, healthy, and skilled. This will necessarily include providing them with a high quality of life. People who must spend large parts of their time struggling for even basic requirements like water or transport to work, and who cannot live in good housing or clean and comfortable surroundings, cannot be productive and healthy participants in society and the economy.

To achieve these developmental goals, the Government will have to create and promote investment in world class infrastructure — power, water, roads, housing, communications and transport. Infrastructure will also have to be created to spur economic growth. This calls for investment on a scale far beyond the resources of the Government, pointing to the need to attract large-scale private investment. To secure this investment, Andhra Pradesh will need to provide a regulatory environment that enables private investment and facilitates business.

The rest of this section explains how these milestones to development will be achieved.

Developing human resources

To make its people secure, skilled and healthy, the State will focus on poverty eradication and social welfare, education, and healthcare.

- *Poverty eradication and social welfare:* The foremost endeavour of the State will be to eradicate poverty. This will be achieved through the following initiatives:

1. *Strengthening public employment schemes:* The objective will be to create a cushion of security by providing the poor with employment. Public employment through works programmes, etc., should be the principal method to provide food security for the poor, 80 per cent of who live in rural areas. This approach will have a double benefit: it will help build rural infrastructure and promote rural development.
2. *Implementing a focused Public Distribution System:* Access to food as a universal entitlement will be a key ingredient in the State's war against hunger and poverty. This goal will be achieved through an effective food security programme. To ensure the sustainability of this effort, the programme will be aimed at clearly identified groups: the poor, vulnerable, and risk-prone.
3. *Launching social security schemes for the aged, disabled, and widowed:* To provide a comprehensive safety net, the State will launch a mix of pension and other schemes for

genuinely vulnerable groups.

4. *Removing current disparities:* The Government will pursue specific strategies to remove disparities between different categories of its people and between different regions of the State. This will include empowering all disadvantaged groups and protecting their rights; continuing with affirmative action to provide them with access to educational and employment opportunities; providing them access to state and civil institutions; and enacting and enforcing legislation that protects the interests of vulnerable groups.

   Backward areas will be developed through a special focus on providing employment and improving development indicators such as education and health.

> The Government will pursue specific strategies to remove disparities between different categories of its people and between different regions of the State.

Exhibit 6 provides an overview of the approach to realising the vision for poverty eradication and social welfare.

Exhibit 6

Poverty Eradication and Social Welfare: Overall Approach to Realising the Vision

Eradicate poverty	• Launch public employment schemes (e.g., rural works programme) to provide minimum livelihood for the unemployed • Design and implement a focused PDS programme to ensure food security for the needy • Launch pension schemes to take care of the aged, disabled and widows
Focus on building capabilities of disadvantaged groups	• Develop specific strategies to improve literacy and health among scheduled castes/tribes, backward classes and minorities • Enact and enforce legislation against child labour and provide access to education for child labourers
Empower women	• Increase gender-sensitisation through training • Address gender inequalities in education and employment • Increase gender-sensititivity in health programmes • Prevent atrocities against women

• *Education:* Education in the State will be strengthened to achieve two aims: universal access to primary education and skill-building. Primary education will be strengthened by providing more schools, managing them better and making teaching more effective. In parallel, secondary and higher education will be augmented, mainly through the provision of courses specifically aimed at equipping students with skills that cater to the needs of the economy and society. Adult literacy programmes will also be pursued to achieve the goal of total literacy by 2010 (Exhibit 7).

Exhibit 7

Education: Overall Approach to Realising the Vision

Ensuring full literacy by 2010	• Ensuring access to primary education for all • Creating demand for education • Focusing on specific groups and districts with low literacy levels
Promoting education among women	• Increasing demand for primary and secondary education among girls • Increasing access to education for girls • Fostering higher education for women
Focusing vocational and higher education on marketable skills	• Providing more options in vocational and technical education at secondary/higher secondary level • Providing more specialised courses in higher education that reflect the needs of the economy and society
Encouraging private sector initiatives in education especially in higher education	• Declaring education an industry • Identifying emerging areas of study • Ensuring quality education through appropriate accreditation and evaluation systems
Creating effective frameworks for managing and funding education	• Putting in place a decentralised participatory management framework (local control through School Committees) • Ensuring government spending is largely directed towards primary and secondary education

• *Health:* To raise health levels, the State will focus on providing universal access to primary healthcare; enhancing secondary and tertiary healthcare and providing affordable access to these services; and strengthening disease prevention programmes. In addition, the State will focus on containing population growth, for instance, through the comprehensive Reproductive and Child Health programme aimed at spreading awareness about family planning and improving the health of women, infants and children (Exhibit 8).

Exhibit 8

HEALTH: OVERALL APPROACH TO REALISING THE VISION

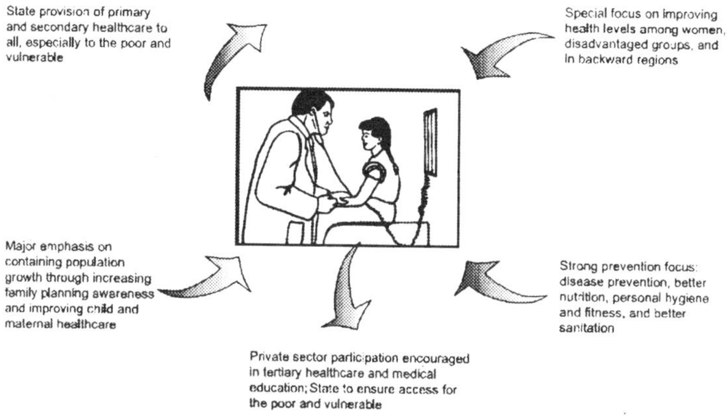

Achieving the development goals outlined above poses a challenge of epic proportions. The Government already spends considerably on education, health and poverty alleviation, and yet has been unable to achieve the desired results. Furthermore, the scale of investment required far exceeds the capacity of Government finance. Thus, the programme for developing Andhra Pradesh's people must incorporate three new approaches: low-cost, innovative solutions; decentralising public services and involving the people in their management; and involving the private sector and development agencies in achieving developmental goals.

• *Low-cost, innovative solutions:* Given the constraints on funding, one strategy to achieve the targets set is to find solutions that are low-cost, innovative, use existing infrastructure and resources, and can be quickly implemented. Three such initiatives are described below.

One way to ensure that every child in Andhra Pradesh gets at least a good basic education is to improve the student-teacher ratio in primary schools. While the State will hire enough teachers to achieve this objective, it will also encourage the more effective use of the services of 'Education Volunteers'. These volunteers will help teachers ensure higher levels of learning in their students, increase enrolment and prevent drop-outs.

Similarly, since creating a formal network of sub-centres to expand the coverage of primary healthcare will be difficult and take a long time to accomplish, the goal can be attained in large part by deploying a network of Community Health Workers (CHWs), backed by a system of referrals to Sub-Centres, throughout the State. CHWs are village residents trained by the Government in providing simple health services. This model has been effective both in experiments in the State (e.g., Rangareddy and Hyderabad districts) and in other parts of the world (e.g., Brazil).

In the same way, rural works programmes could provide minimum employment to the unemployed poor (as explained earlier) and, thus, a more cost-effective solution to providing food security for them. While making them productively employed, such programmes would also create local assets like roads and minor irrigation systems.

• *Involving the people in managing services:* Experience has shown that a good way to make services efficient and responsive is to decentralise them and ensure that the people have a role in managing them.

Many countries have decentralised the management of public services. In the late 70s, Chile decentralised the government healthcare system by devolving responsibility to local government. Budget and personnel responsibilities were transferred to municipalities, which began to operate and control primary healthcare services. Closer home, Andhra Pradesh's own experiment in water management demonstrates the power of people's participation. School Committees have been granted the right to help manage primary schools.

The 73rd and 74th Constitutional Amendments already provide for the devolution of power and responsibilities to local government. Also, the State's own legislation in relation to local bodies provides some basis for people's participation. The principal challenge is to make these frameworks operational.

• *Attracting the private sector and development agencies:* While the Government will always remain the provider of essential services like basic education and health, it cannot and should not remain the sole provider of all such services. Experience all over the world has shown that the private sector, operating in a competitive situation, is better able than governments to provide efficient, rationally priced and high quality services in many areas. The State's support in such areas should gradually be limited to ensuring access for the poor to these services.

The introduction of private sector participation will not only provide the people with better quality and affordable services, it will free Government resources and attention for higher priority developmental goals. Investment by the private sector, for instance in higher education and specialised healthcare, will be substantially increased to lighten the budgetary pressure on the Government.

In addition, the Government will secure assistance from international development agencies such as the World Bank and the Department for International Development (DFID). In Korea, for instance, aid from international agencies played a critical role in providing primary education.

Providing a high quality of life

To raise the quality of life for its people, the State will need to make its villages and cities better places to live in by ensuring that they have clean air and water, services such as sanitation and waste management, and infrastructure, such as power, housing, and transport.

Most of the approaches outlined in the previous section apply equally to making Andhra Pradesh a better place to live: providing basic services; ensuring compliance with minimum environmental standards; finding low cost solutions; leveraging private funds; and involving local communities in the management of services.

• *Providing basic services:* Andhra Pradesh will commit itself to providing basic civic services such as water, sanitation, housing and transport to all its people throughout the State. The Government will use a mix of local and State funding, depending on local resources, to set up basic services.

• *Making environmental concerns an integral part of development planning:* Andhra Pradesh will plan the use and management of its environmental resources in an integrated way, ensure that environmental standards are based on the carrying capacity of a region, and internalise environmental considerations in policy-making. The State will also encourage compliance with standards through market-based enforcement mechanisms.

• *Finding low cost solutions:* Several options exist to innovate and create low cost models for setting up civic services. For instance, the conventional, standardised sanitation system need not be built everywhere. NGOs in West Bengal have developed a menu of lower cost options, costing less than a fifth of the current system. Local communities could choose models they can afford and upgrade them over time.

• *Utilising private sector funds:* The world over, cities access capital markets in many ways to create urban infrastructure: municipalities issue municipal bonds (as has been done in Ahmedabad recently); urban utilities are created that access capital markets like any other private company; private operators participate in setting up specific services like solid waste management and effluent treatment plants. The State's municipalities will actively explore such opportunities to bring in private sector funds.

• *Involving local communities:* Civic services and environmental standards are local issues, best monitored and managed by local governments and users' associations. The Government will, therefore, empower local governments to manage services and create the mechanisms for local communities to articulate their demands. It will also need to provide the financial and technical support local governments and communities will need to effectively play this role.

The Government will empower local governments to manage services and create the mechanisms for local communities to articulate their demands.

Exhibit 9 explains how a paradigm shift in environment management can make Andhra Pradesh clean and green. Exhibit 10 lays out strategies to improve the quality of life in urban areas while Exhibit 11 outlines an integrated approach to improving the quality of life in rural Andhra Pradesh.

Exhibit 9

A Paradigm Shift in Environment Management

From	To
• Lack of integrated environmental planning (e.g., policies do not always internalise environmental considerations)	• Integrated environmental resources planning: State creates an integrated plan for conserving and utilising environmental resources and determines the 'carrying capacity' of each individual region. Policy makers use the resources plan and internalise it in their policies/projects
• Development in a region takes place with scant regard to the 'carrying capacity' of the region. No stakeholder involvement in setting environmental standards	• Area-based standards based on carrying capacity of the zone are set for each zone by involving all primary stakeholders (e.g., NGOs, industry, local government, etc.)
• Compliance monitoring is centralised and enforcement mechanism is not market-based, i.e., not based on incentive mechanisms	• Market-based regulation is used as enforcement mechanism. Local committees/community are empowered to monitor compliance with standards

Promoting investment

To attract private investment, the State will first need to create the conditions that will allow private investors to successfully participate in its development. This involves building infrastructure and reforming regulation to create a conducive environment for business.

Exhibit 10

APPROACH TO IMPROVING THE QUALITY OF URBAN LIFE

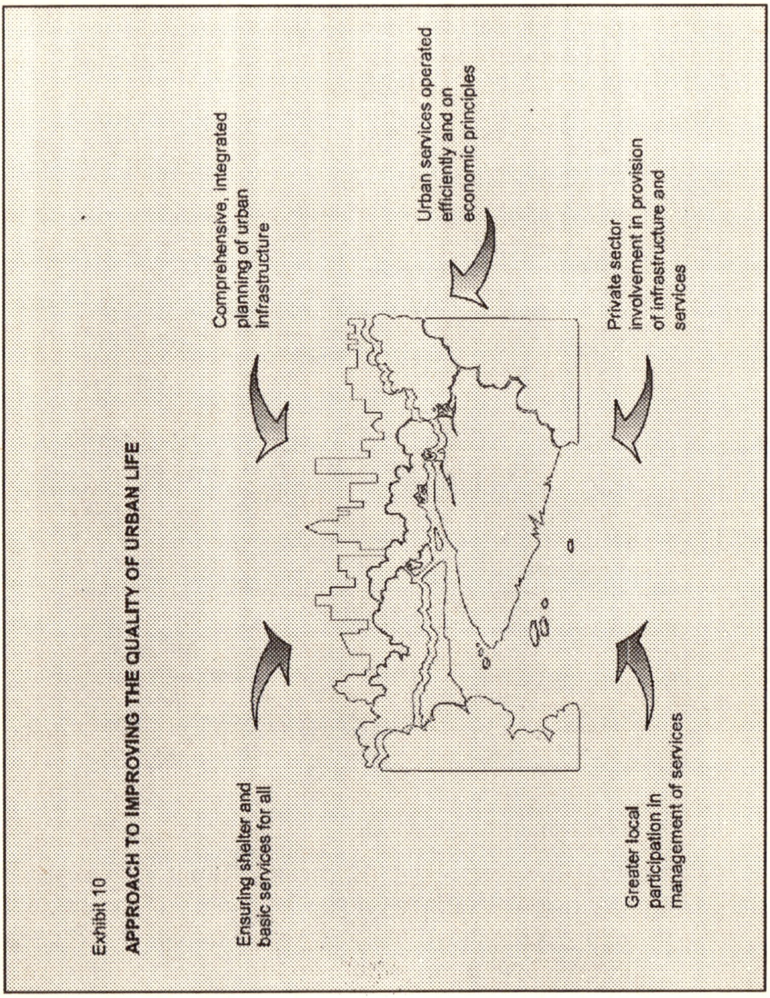

Exhibit 11

Approach to Improving Rural Standards of Living

Approach to improving rural standard of living	Agricultural development and reforms	• Integrated development of rain-fed areas • Watershed development/irrigation; harnessing water resources • Shift from agriculture for subsistence to agriculture for economic gain • Waste and marginal lands brought into productive use • Use of technology for optimum productivity and quality
	Creation of economic opportunities in rural industry and services	• Identifying and promoting opportunities in rural services • Building awareness about alternative economic opportunities • Providing access to low cost finance to promote entrepreneurship • Introducing community banking (participatory) to increase capacity to handle resources and avoid stress in times of emergency
	Provision of rural infrastructure	• Encouraging self-help in identifying needs, developing and managing local infrastructure, and ensuring connectivity to urban centres • Ensuring availability of finance and technical assistance
	Human resources development and capability building	• Ensuring universal literacy by 2010 • Building skills to match economic opportunities • Focusing on disease prevention • Increasing awareness of family planning options • Providing universal access to primary healthcare • Focusing on development of women, youth and children • Introducing technology to remove drudgery and improve efficiency and productivity
	Decentralised governance and promotion of self-help groups	• Ensuring fiscal and administative decentralisation • Undertaking large scale campaigns to increase awareness of people's rights and duties-shift from programme to process approach • Fostering community participation through self-help groups • Providing training in financial prudence, building administrative skills and increasing IT literacy

Infrastructure of three types, trunk, specialised and arterial, will need to be created. Trunk infrastructure comprising roads, ports, airports, power, etc., is required to connect key economic centres. For instance, expressways connecting Hyderabad, Warangal, Karimnagar, Visakhapatnam, Nellore, Vijayawada and Anantpur will have to be constructed. Communications links between these cities and to other Indian states will have to be created. Creating trunk infrastructure will be one of the State's main priorities.

In parallel, Andhra Pradesh will need to build specialised infrastructure, such as cold storage facilities for fresh produce or large scale cargo movement facilities. Finally, arterial infrastructure connecting key economic centres and rural areas to the growth corridors must be constructed in tandem with the building of trunk infrastructure to ensure that the benefits of development are spread throughout the State.

Building trunk and arterial infrastructure alone, on the scale required, calls for an investment of over Rs.4,00,000 crore till 2010 (over Rs.16,00,000 crore till 2020). While the Government will invest in infrastructure much more than in the past, it will not be able to raise these funds on its own. Fortunately, it will not need to. Considerable funds are available from international sources. In 1996 alone, international investment in infrastructure in developing countries amounted to Rs.1,00,000 crore. Non-Resident Indians are another source of private investment. The Government will need to extensively tap these sources. However, before it can involve the private sector in infrastructure building, the Government will need to create the necessary conditions for its participation. These include rationalising pricing; creating a new regulatory framework; and restructuring government infrastructure agencies.

• *Rationalising pricing:* Pricing in the infrastructure sector currently does not reflect the true economic cost of providing goods or services. But without rational pricing, the Government cannot continue to provide these services economically and neither can the private sector be induced to provide them. Rationalising pricing is thus a critical element in attracting private sector participation. However, while introducing such reform, to avoid hardship to weaker sections, the Government will continue to provide subsidies where necessary.

• *Creating a new regulatory framework:* The Government will need to provide an appropriate regulatory framework to enable private sector participation in infrastructure development. For example, autonomous bodies will need to be set up to determine tariffs and set quality standards for services. Andhra Pradesh can draw on the experience of countries like the Philippines, Malaysia and Argentina to develop a new framework for the infrastructure sector.

• *Restructuring government infrastructure agencies:* Government infrastructure agencies will need to operate autonomously and efficiently and, where possible, be subject to the same rules of competition as the private sector. For instance, these agencies should compete on an equitable basis with independent power producers to supply power to the grid. Such competition will breed efficiency, reduce costs and improve services. In addition, Government agencies will need to develop the skills to compete, and become performance-focused. Some of these institutions could also be progressively privatised, keeping public interest in view. The distribution and generation segments of Andhra Pradesh's electricity sector are cases in point. Andhra Pradesh could draw on international experience to manage this transition.

To further increase the State's attractiveness to investors, the Government will also need to simplify its procedure for approvals. The State Investment Promotion Board to expedite government clearances is a step in this direction. Going forward, the Government will need to undertake additional initiatives to simplify procedures such as creating cross-ministry investment promotion boards that minimise the number of decision-makers and steps involved.

Section 1 of this document spells out the approach to each element of the programme to build capabilities in the State: poverty eradication and social welfare, education, health, urban and rural development, environment, infrastructure and deregulation.

FOCUSING ON SELECT GROWTH ENGINES

To achieve the 9-10 per cent growth targeted, the State will need to stimulate economic growth by focusing on specific sectors that offer high growth opportunities. These will be the growth engines of the economy: dynamic and fast growing agricultural, services and manufacturing enterprises. They will be the primary growth engines of the economy because they will contribute a sizeable part of the State's GSDP (Gross State Domestic Product) and employment.

> To achieve the 9-10 per cent growth targeted, the State will need to stimulate economic growth by focusing on specific sectors that offer high growth opportunities.

Andhra Pradesh will focus on 19 primary growth engines: six in agriculture; six in industry; and seven in services. They are :

- Rice, poultry, dairy, horticulture, agro-industry and fisheries in agriculture.
- Construction, mining-based industries, labour-intensive export-oriented industries (e.g., garments and leather products), pharmaceuticals, small-scale industry and infrastructure in industry.
- Basic information technology services, knowledge-based services, logistics, tourism, small-scale services, healthcare and education in services.

Infrastructure, healthcare, and education are important because of their role in building capabilities. However, as experience in developed countries has shown, these sectors can be highly revenue- and employment-generating and are therefore growth engines in their own right.

It is not useful to try to project how much each growth engine will contribute towards achieving the growth targets for each sector of the economy. For instance, 15 years ago, it would have been impossible to forecast the levels of growth the software and IT industries are now bringing to the Indian economy. What is pertinent, therefore, is to unleash the growth potential in important areas and create sustainable, high annual growth.

The focus on these growth engines does not mean that other important sectors such as engineering-based industries or financial services will not flourish. On the contrary, they will continue to grow, benefiting from the State's overall approach to and investments in improving the economy in general.

How were these growth engines identified? How will they create economic growth? What does the State Government need to do to facilitate the development of the growth engines?

The rest of this section answers these questions.

Identifying the growth engines

Each growth engine satisfies at least one of the following criteria: it builds on the State's strengths; it has the potential to create great economic impact; it can capture opportunities created by global trends.

• *Builds on the State's strengths:* In a globally competitive world, each region has to exploit its comparative advantage to maximise economic opportunity. Western Australia, for example, has exploited its significant mineral wealth to develop one of the most competitive, technologically advanced mining industries in the world. New Zealand has used its large pasture lands to great advantage to build an efficient, cost-competitive, large-scale and export-oriented dairy industry that corners as much as 30 per cent of the world dairy trade. Malaysia has used its low labour costs to become a key centre for global electronics assembly. And Singapore has effectively used its strategic location (at the centre of the world's major shipping routes) to become a major trading centre and an international logistics hub, linking Asia to the rest of the world.

• *Has the potential for significant economic impact:* The growth engines need to be large and high growth industries. Furthermore, to ensure that growth is equitable, they should have the potential to generate large-scale employment. China, for example, has focused on the manufacture of export-oriented, labourintensive goods like garments, leather products, and toys. With exports amounting to nearly $50 billion, these industries are now a key element of China's economic growth. More importantly, they have generated large-scale employment for China's vast pool of workers.

• *Builds on opportunities created by global trends:* The

expansion of global trade has created tremendous opportunities. Singapore, the Netherlands, and the US recognised this trend early and built major trade and logistics centres in their countries. By taking advantage of India's increasing participation in global trade and its geographic position, Andhra Pradesh will similarly innovate to create India's premier logistics centre.

Another.key trend is at work: computing and communications technologies are overriding the limitations of physical distance, allowing many services to be provided remotely (that is, far away from the customer/patron of the service) and spawning entirely new and exciting IT-based industries. An increased emphasis on knowledge and a trend towards knowledge-based industries and services is pushing the limits of research and its applications, for example in biotechnology, and genetic science. Israel has leveraged its scientific talent to build a strong presence in Information Technology and biotechnology. Korea and the Philippines are taking advantage of increased connectivity to provide remote services in animation and entertainment to US-based corporations. And Malaysia has already set up an ambitious project – the Multimedia Supercorridor – to become a key player in the global IT and multimedia arena. Andhra Pradesh's IT and Knowledge Corridor initiatives are aimed at ensuring the high penetration of information technology services and telecommunications and developing new and rapidly growing industries.

Finally, global deregulation and the opening up of markets are creating opportunities for many other industries. The reduction and ultimate removal of quotas (with the phasing out of the Multi-Fibre Agreement) will create opportunities in garment manufacturing and exports. Greater adherence to Intellectual Property Rights will boost remote R&D services and pharmaceuticals manufacturing in India. Reduction in agricultural subsidies the world over will increase trade in agricultural commodities like rice.

In line with this approach, the rest of this section lays out the criteria behind the selection of each of the 19 primary growth engines identified in agriculture, industry and services.

1. Agriculture:

Andhra Pradesh will follow a comprehensive strategy to achieve agricultural growth. This will include harnessing water resources, developing agriculture in rain-fed areas, spurring growth through agricultural reform, and developing high potential areas which can be agricultural growth engines. The rationale for the agriculture growth engines is as follows:

Rice

Rice is such a large contributor to Andhra Pradesh's economy (contributing a quarter of agricultural GSDP) that even small improvements in the sector will create a large impact. Since rice-growing is the primary occupation of a large proportion of the State's agricultural labour, its further development will increase rural incomes and reduce poverty. Andhra Pradesh is very well placed to develop this sector. Its climate is well suited to growing rice and it is already one of the top three Indian states in rice production.

Dairy

Dairy is a very large market in India (around Rs.80,000 crore) and is expected to grow at 15 per cent a year due to the high income elasticity of dairy products[3]. Large growth potential will also emerge once export markets open up through the World Trade Organisation (WTO) agreements. Developing this sector will have significant economic impact since it will create many jobs, particularly for rural women.

Poultry

The poultry sector is large and likely to grow at 15 per cent over the next 10 years. This growth can create many higher income jobs in semi-rural areas. Again, Andhra Pradesh is well placed to develop its poultry sector: it is already the largest producer of eggs and poultry meat in the country and a significant producer of maize, a major input in poultry feed.

Horticulture

The markets for fresh produce and processed foods are likely to grow considerably for two reasons. First, consumption will

3. Demand is said to be income elastic when even small increases in income give rise to large increases in consumption.

increase steadily as incomes rise with development. Second, exports potential will grow considerably once subsidies are eliminated and tariffs are rationalised under WTO agreements. As the second largest producer of fruits and one of the largest producers of vegetables in the country, Andhra Pradesh can create a strong position in domestic and export markets.

Fisheries

Andhra Pradesh has rich fishery potential in inland, marine and brackish water fisheries. The State has the second largest coastline among Indian states (974) km and a continental shelf of 33,227 square km; a river course of over 8,500 km; and large fresh water and brackish water lakes. Brackish water areas are estimated to exceed 150,000 hectares. The development of this sector will create considerable impact, particularly by providing livelihoods for the poor.

Agro-industry

Andhra Pradesh can capitalise on its agricultural advantages to further develop its agro-industries using raw materials such as cotton, sugar, tobacco, chillies, etc. Furthermore, agro-industry can create considerable economic impact through value addition, higher export earnings, and high employment, especially in rural areas.

2. Industry:

Expanding infrastructure, focusing on skill-building and simplifying procedures will be major elements in developing the industry growth engines. The growth engines that will create the highest economic impact in the short term are infrastructure and construction. Export-oriented garments and leather products industries, pharmaceuticals and mining and mineral processing will also be attractive opportunities in the medium term.

Infrastructure

To jump-start economic growth, the State will need to focus on building infrastructure, the primary enabler of growth. Infrastructure development will have a tremendous impact on Andhra Pradesh's economy. The building of infrastructure will itself create large scale employment. Once constructed, the maintenance of this infrastructure and infrastructure services (e.g., running power plants) will also create jobs and thus income. But for Andhra Pradesh, the greatest impact of infrastructure development will come from its multiplier effect on the economy, i.e., the boost it will provide to the output and productivity of other industries. Furthermore, if Andhra Pradesh builds infrastructure on the scale required, it will be able to attract a disproportionate share of private investment, thereby creating even more jobs and income for its people.

Construction

Construction offers huge growth potential and economic impact. The sector will experience strong growth due to the construction boom that will follow the impetus to infrastructure creation. This growth will have a strong multiplier effect, i.e., it will create demand for industries like steel, cement, glass, etc., which are critical inputs in the building of plants, factories, and other infrastructure. All these activities will create many jobs for skilled labour.

Garments and Leather Products

A focus on this sector will allow Andhra Pradesh to capitalise on its competitive labour costs and its long coastline (providing easy access to export markets). In fact, the major opportunity is in exports, particularly from falling trade barriers and the dismantling of quotas (for garments). Since these are labour-intensive industries, a focus on them will also create large-scale employment.

Mining

Infrastructure development is creating tremendous demand for the State's key minerals, coal and limestone. Both are key inputs in power generation and construction. The State can capitalise on its rich deposits of these minerals, and of others like bauxite, to build a strong position in this sector. This will create considerable impact in terms of contribution to GSDP and job creation.

Pharmaceuticals

Andhra Pradesh has a considerable base and expertise in bulk drugs. It also has several pharmaceuticals- and life-sciences based R&D institutions. This will allow the State to capitalise on the opportunities that will emerge after India's patent regime changes in 2005. Apart from becoming a thriving production and R&D centre, the State will benefit from the large demand worldwide for low cost generics formulations and bulk drugs.

Small-scale industries

Andhra Pradesh has a strong small-scale manufacturing sector which has the potential to create significant employment and self-employment opportunities in the State. Small-scale industries are much more flexible, respond faster, and embrace innovation more quickly than large industries. Given the important role of small-scale manufacturing in the development of economies such as the US, the State recognises the importance of developing this sector as a part of its growth programme.

3. Services:

Given the evolution of economies worldwide towards a dominant services sector, services offer huge potential for growth. Andhra Pradesh has already made a strong start in developing the Information Technology sector; this should now be expanded to other knowledge areas like biotechnology. Services growth engines also include tourism, logistics, small-scale services, healthcare and education.

Information Technology

The IT industry will experience explosive growth due to the increasing importance of IT in business and society and India's strengths in this sector. The productivity gains from increased IT usage will create a huge impact on the economy. By building on its considerable strengths in IT and its large and growing number of IT professionals, Andhra Pradesh will be able to capture the huge opportunity available through the global shift towards electronic commerce as well as the increasing importance of IT in every sphere of the economy.

Knowledge-based services

More and more countries are focusing on knowledge and skill development as a source of sustainable growth. Andhra Pradesh has considerable potential to create a Knowledge Corridor, i.e., an area equipped to foster research and development and the commercialisation of newly developed technologies. Research in areas like biotechnology, advanced materials, and cutting-edge industrial technologies provide attractivc opportunities. In addition, several options to develop a centre for knowledge-based remote services using IT networks are also emerging.

Tourism

Tourism can be a major money-spinner and foreign exchange earner. It also generates large-scale employment, particularly in small services. Andhra Pradesh has strengths here as well such as its historical, religious, and leisure sites, existing or potential, on which it can build a considerable tourism sector. Other strengths include the State's central location in India and its long coastline.

Logistics

Economic growth will lead to increased global trade and the movement of goods within India. Andhra Pradesh will use its central location in the country and its long coastline to attract a large share of the opportunities created through this trend.

Small-scale services

A thriving small-scale services segment will provide significant employment opportunities in higher value added jobs, particularly in rural and semi-rural areas. The growth of this sector will thus enable the occupational shift and productive employment of Andhra Pradesh's large number of agricultural labourers, a large proportion of whom are under-employed.

Healthcare

Healthcare will become a large market once different levels (secondary and tertiary healthcare) and different areas (e.g., health insurance) are opened up to private investment and competition, and the Government's budgetary support to this sector increases. Again, this will increase the prosperity of Andhra Pradesh's people by creating a large number of jobs.

Education

The huge need for and emphasis on technical and vocational education will make this sector a significant engine of growth. Its development will also create employment throughout the State.

The process of identifying and developing growth engines is a dynamic one. The State will need to re-prioritise its thrust areas as its competitive strengths change over time. For example, in the 1970s, Taiwan leveraged its twin advantages of low labour costs and central Pacific location/coastline to build a strong global position in export-oriented, low-technology, labour-intensive industries. But today its labour costs are no longer competitive, and so Taiwan has switched its focus to knowledgebased industries. Similarly, Andhra Pradesh may need to de-emphasise some areas and emphasise others as it moves up the ladder of economic development.

Andhra Pradesh is not the only State or country pursuing high growth in sectors with attractive opportunities. For instance, at least six Indian states have the stated goal of becoming forces in the IT industry. Many south-east Asian countries with lower currency values will be aggressive in labour intensive sectors like garments and leather products.

Thus, while Andhra Pradesh has chosen growth engines based on its current competitiveness, it has also resolved to achieve two objectives. First, in areas where other states or countries are stronger but not dominant, Andhra Pradesh will maintain a sharp focus and high responsiveness to investor needs in an all-out effort to catch up with or overtake its competitors (as it is doing in IT services). Second, in other areas, such as logistics and knowledge-based services, Andhra Pradesh will aim to innovate quickly, before other states do so.

How the growth engines will stimulate growth

The focus on growth engines will stimulate economic growth by rapidly increasing the productivity of Andhra Pradesh's labour; creating a more substantial exports thrust; and building on regional strengths. Located in all the three regions of Andhra Pradesh, their growth will ensure regionally balanced development. To maximise the use of scarce resources, they will be concentrated in centres or 'clusters' connected by 'growth corridors'. Furthermore, the growth engines will create growth in differing time frames, with infrastructure and construction being the principal growth engines in the short term, i.e., the first five years of the growth thrust.

• *The productivity of labour will be rapidly increased:* Productive use of costcompetitive labour has proved a considerable stimulus to the growth of several high growth Asian economies. Japan, Korea, China, Malaysia and Taiwan, for example, have used their large numbers of semi-skilled workers (and an emphasis on quality) to build successful garments, leather products and electronics industries. India itself has used its competent and cost-competitive knowledge workers[4] to build software exports. India, and Andhra Pradesh, have an exceptional opportunity to grow through the productive use of labour, particularly since labour costs here are among the most competitive in the world (Exhibit 12) and the scope to raise the productivity of a significant part of the workforce is large. Andhra Pradesh will, therefore, rapidly improve the productivity of its workforce by building its people's skills, transferring technology from world class companies, and providing infrastructure comparable to the best in the world.

Exhibit 12

India's Labour Costs are among the most Competitive in the World

Hourly labour cost in the apparel industry: US $

Developed countries	Japan Germany France USA USA UK
Newly industrialised nations	Taiwan Hong Kong Singapore South Korea Malaysia
South-East Asian nations	Thailand Philippines Indonesia
China and Sourth Asian countries	Sri Lanka India China Bangladesh

* April 1998

Source: Werner International Management Consultants; Asian Development Bank; Internet, McKinsey analysis

• *Export-led growth will receive more focus:* India, in the past, has not sufficiently emphasised export-led growth, focusing instead on import substitution. However, to achieve and sustain 9-10 per cent growth, a focus on exports is critical for several reasons.

First, in many of the growth engines, the domestic market alone may not be large enough to create significant economic opportunity. A case in point is processed fruit or vegetable products. Indian markets for these products today are very small and unlikely to grow to a significant size very quickly. However, there is a large export market for these items; in fact, processed fruits and vegetables account for 90 per cent of the international trade in fruits and vegetables. Second, in many areas, the export market may be more attractive than the domestic market. For example, in garments and IT services, realisations from international sales can be many times higher than those from domestic sales. Third, exporting necessarily means producing goods and services of internationally accepted standards. To be internationally competitive, therefore, export-oriented firms would acquire modern technology, develop an efficient and low-cost procurement base, invest in efficient logistics systems, develop quality control systems, and focus on customer service and innovation. This will have a positive effect on other sectors of the economy as domestic firms emulate export-oriented firms on all these counts.

> The growth engines identified for Andhra Pradesh are located throughout its three regions: Telangana, Andhra, and Rayalaseema, and build upon their natural and historical strengths

• *Every region's strengths would be utilised:* The growth engines are chosen to maximise the potential of each region. Thus, the growth engines identified for Andhra Pradesh are located throughout its three regions: Telangana, Andhra, and Rayalaseema, and build upon their natural and historical strengths (Exhibit 13). For instance, Telangana's strengths in maize production and horticulture make it a good location for the poultry, horticulture,

4 Individuals with specialised knowledge and skills in fields like software, medicine, accounting, etc.

and agro-industry growth engines. Its tourist attractions and IT-literate workforce will support the development of the tourism and IT growth engines. Andhra's extensive coastline makes it possible to locate the logistics and distribution hub around its three cities: Vijayawada, Visakhapatnam and Kakinada. Its skilled labour force and strengths in horticulture and rice will support the garments and leather products, horticulture, and rice growth engines. The Rayalaseema region is a natural choice for mining and quarrying because of its large limestone and granite deposits. As in the other two regions, its strengths in horticulture and low labour costs make it a good location for horticulture and labour-intensive, export-oriented industries.

Exhibit 13

The Growth Engines Leverage the Strengths of Andhra Pradesh's Three Main Regions

Telangana

Strengths	*Growth engines*
* Minerals (e.g., coal)	* Mining-based activities
* Strong maize production base	* Poultry/Agro-processing
* Horticulture (e.g., grapes)	* Agro-processing/ Horticulture
* Tourist attractions (Nagarjunasagar, Nizam culture)	* Tourism
* Competitive labour costs	* Labour-intensive, export-oriented industries
* Educated, IT-literate labour force (Hyderabad)	* IT/Knowledge corridor

Rayalaseema

Stengths	**Growth engines**
* Limestone, granite/ building materials	* Mining (quarrying)-based activity
* Horticulture base (variety of fruits/ vegetables)	* Agro-processing/ Horticulture
* Tourist attractions	* Tourism (e.g., Tirupati)
* Competitive labour costs	* Labour-intensive, export-oriented industries

Andhra

Strengths	Growth engines
* Minerals (bauxite, granite)	* Mining-based activity/mineral processing
* Horticulture (Mangoes, chillies)	* Agro-processing Horticulture
* Irrigated rice-growing land	* Rice
* Long coastline	* Logistics hub, fisheries
* Competitive labour costs	* Labour-intensive export-oriented industries
* Fodder availability	* Dairy
* Tourist attractions (e.g., beaches)	* Tourism

• Growth will be propelled by 'clusters' of development connected by 'growth corridors': Andhra Pradesh's growth engines will best be developed by focusing efforts in geographically concentrated 'clusters'. Clusters are groups of mutually reinforcing and supporting industries. Italy's textiles cluster, for instance, comprises not merely fabric and garment manufacture but also supporting industries like textile machinery and design, all located within a compact 200-300 sq. km. Competitive industries develop not in isolation but in such clusters that allow close co-operation between companies and so boost their competitiveness.

The clusters created will need to be connected by 'corridors' of transport and communications infrastructure. Roads, telecommunications links, industrial estates, ports and airports should form parts of the corridor. These corridors will reinforce trade between clusters. The clusters and corridors approach makes it possible to make the best use of scarce resources by concentrating them initially on select areas, and creating critical mass and high quality. The development of these clusters and corridors will spearhead the development and spread of economic activity in all parts of the State[5].

Major clusters in the State will be Hyderabad, Karimnagar, Warangal, Tirupati, Visakhapatnam, Vijayawada, Anantpur and Nellore. These clusters will be connected to other major Indian citiesùDelhi, Mumbai, Bangalore, Chennai, Calcutta and Bhopalùto facilitate economic activity between states.

• *Infrastructure and construction will be the principal growth engines in the immediate future:* Building infrastructure is a prerequisite for the development of most of the growth engines and will therefore be a top priority over the next five years. Over Rs.4,00,000 crore[6] will need to be invested till 2010 in building infrastructure. This alone will stimulate growth by creating considerable employment and income in the State. Once infrastructure is built, its operation will continue to generate significant income. Today, operating infrastructure, as in

5 In other words, this approach will not lead to development only around the clusters and corridors. The growth programmes will require infrastructure development in rural areas, education and health initiatives, and improvement in civic services, across the State. Also, the development of agriculture growth engines and smallscale services will spread economic benefits across the State.

6 At constant 1995-96 prices.

maintaining roads and running power plants, creates a larger proportion of income in developed economies than in developing ones. Furthermore, the construction industry will be a major beneficiary of the thrust to build infrastructure: tremendous business and employment opportunities will be generated in building roads, power plants, industrial parks, ports, irrigation systems, and so on.

This emphasis on infrastructure as a driver of growth is consistent with the approaches of countries like China. China plans to attract investment of as much as $100 billion in infrastructure in the next few years. It expects activity in this sector to create considerable employment for its people.

The development of many of the growth engines will be constrained until the requisite infrastructure is created; it could be ten or more years before many industries have the infrastructure they require. Therefore, sectors, which do not depend heavily on infrastructure creation for growth, such as agriculture and services, are likely to develop faster and drive early growth.

How the State Government will catalyse the development of the growth engines

While the growth engines will be developed mainly by private investment, the Government will have a major role to play in catalysing their development. One of its first tasks will be to attract private investors to help build the growth engines. To do this, the Government will need to create the conditions that will allow players to build profitable businesses in the State.

This will require action on four fronts: (1) providing infrastructure; (2) deregulating or creating regulation that fosters investment and facilitates business; (3) accelerating the development of skills; and (4) conducting focused and effective promotion to market the opportunities the State offers to investors.

• *Providing specialised[7] infrastructure:* Currently, the growth of many sectors identified as growth engines is severely constrained because they lack critical infrastructure. For example, in horticulture, the lack of adequate post-harvesting facilitiesùcold storage; cleaning, grading and packing facilities; refrigerated transport — causes around 25-30 per cent of the fruits, vegetables and flowers produced every year to rot.

In other sectors, future growth and expansion will be possible only if current infrastructure is upgraded and expanded. For example, to make Hyderabad an IT mega-hub, a broadband digital highway is a basic requirement. This entails a manifold increase in bandwidth from the current 2 Mb network in the State.

Entirely new infrastructure will have to be built to drive growth in areas where Andhra Pradesh has little or no base. A well-developed exports processing zone will have to be established close to a port to facilitate the development of exportoriented garments and leather products industries. To build a world class logistics hub, large container terminals at Visakhapatnam and Kakinada ports with an intermodal container transfer facility will be needed, among other things. Developing new mines will require dedicated rail links between the mining area and the consumption area.

Specialised infrastructure can be built by the State, by the private sector, or jointly by the two. However, in all cases, the State will actively facilitate its development.

> To allow marketbased growth and to prudently regulate this growth, the State must create favourable regulation and simplify procedures.

• *Deregulating or creating regulation that fosters investment and facilitates business:* To allow market-based growth and to prudently regulate this growth, the State must create favourable regulation and simplify procedures for investors. Many laws have to be scrapped or significantly modified; many have to be strengthened, supplemented and have their enforcement procedures spelled out. In some areas, new laws and policies will have to be formulated. Regulatory change of this order will not be possible

7 To achieve the targeted growth levels, infrastructure of the following types will need to be built: trunk, i.e., roads, ports, airports, power, etc.; specialised, e.g., high-speed telecommunication links, cold storage; and arterial, e.g., smaller roads and telecommunication links connecting villages and towns to key economic centres.

without the Centre's participation and co-operation. Therefore, to create a favourable regulatory climate, the State will not only have to undertake significant initiatives at the State level but also influence the Centre to act. The initiatives should take the following form:

First, the State must identify and eliminate outdated laws that constrain growth. For example, it needs to review the reservation of certain industries for the smallscale sector (e.g., leather and garments). This has inhibited the modernisation and technological upgrading of these industries adversely affecting their competitiveness in quality and cost[8]. De-reserving industries will allow competitive players to enter and make the kinds of investment necessary to develop the industries. To enable small-scale industries to become competitive, the Government will help them to upgrade their technology and skills.

The State must also modify existing laws, particularly to reduce discretionary elements, or formulate new ones. For example, the State should strengthen the policy framework to facilitate private sector participation in developing unexploited resources and reform regulation to enable wasteland development.

In particular, the State must strengthen or formulate laws that protect the public interest (such as laws relating to environmental pollution and quality certification). To illustrate, the State will need to formulate a clear policy on mining to ensure the sustainable development of Andhra Pradesh's mineral resources.

Second, the State will need to develop strong, innovative enforcement mechanisms that are fair and transparent. These are crucial for creating confidence in investors about the efficacy of the State's (and the country's) laws and the State's commitment to provide a facilitating regulatory environment. They are also critical for protecting the environment and the interests of the people. For example, to enforce the regulation on environmentally sustainable mining, the State could consider introducing such provisions as

---

8 India is perhaps the only country to reserve manufacturing sectors for small-scale ventures. To become globally competitive, India will have to revise this policy. Doing so may reduce opportunities in some sectors to smallscale players, but new ones will open up in the services sector (see Chapter 27, The Bonanza in Small-Scale Services). The challenge for Andhra Pradesh will be to re-train its workforce to take advantage of the new opportunities.

'performance bonds' (bank guaranteed security deposits) through which an enterprise would guarantee restoration of mined areas. The deposits should be kept marginally higher than the restoration cost to provide an economic incentive for restoring the mined land. The Western Australia government has used this technique to ensure environmentally sustainable mining activity.

Third, to encourage investment in the growth engines, the State will specifically aim to simplify and rationalise procedures and clearances for these sectors. For example, land identification and acquisition/leasing procedures for agroindustries (which require large tracts of semi-agricultural land) need to be simplified and facilitated.

The Government has recently taken some steps to simplify procedures. For example, it has set up the State Investment Promotion Board which has significantly reduced the time needed to obtain specific clearances. Similarly, the Andhra Pradesh Industrial Infrastructure Corporation has earmarked land for industrial estates to reduce inconvenience in identifying and acquiring projectsuitable land. However, to achieve dramatic growth, the Government will have to do much more. First, it will need to cultivate a mindset of æpartnership' with private investors and consult them in setting policies and procedures for the State. Second, it will need to introduce wide-reaching measures to simplify and hasten approvals mainly by cutting down the vast number of regulations that currently apply. Mexico used a fairly radical approach to doing this. A 'deregulation czar' was appointed; any citizen wanting a regulation to be discarded could approach the 'czar'. This official was obliged to review the regulation and give a decision within 45 days. If no decision was forthcoming at the end of this period, the regulation was automatically scrapped.

• *Accelerating the development of skills:* To develop the growth engines, existing skills will have to be upgraded and new skills will have to be created. In addition, skills and research developed in laboratories and classrooms must be efficiently transferred to the State's fields and factories, so that the benefits of superior skills and technology are realised.

To build marketable skills, a large number of vocational training schools providing industry-specific training programmes will be opened and popularised. As a first step, these schools will be set up in large numbers across the State so that the number of trained workers is greatly increased. In addition, the network of Industrial Training Institutes and polytechnics will be significantly expanded to produce skilled workers such as the large number of construction supervisors and other personnel needed to support the growth of the construction industry. Second, these technical schools will offer a variety of training programmes so that diverse skills can be developed. For instance, training institutions for construction-related trades like masonry, welding, etc., today offer training programmes only in a few trades; they will begin to offer training in many more. Third, the training programmes offered will incorporate training on the latest technologies so that skills can be constantly upgraded. And last, the State will have to set up apex training institutes that train and certify skilled workers as trainers. These trainers can then set up a network of institutes with certification from the apex training institute.

To build new skills and to develop R&D relevant to industry, unique institutions offering specialised education and research facilities need to be set up. The Indian Institute of Information Technology is a step in this direction. Andhra Pradesh will aim to become the 'Education Capital of India' by building 15 to 20 unique educational institutions in the State through affiliations with important universities worldwide. Some of these will be first rate research institutions, on the lines of the Massachusetts Institute of Technology and Stanford University in the USA, while some will be vocational training institutes.

The three-pronged approach of facilitating cutting edge research and development, high quality education and entrepreneurial start-ups, has worked very well to create new industries in the US. Countries like the UK, Germany, and Taiwan are now trying to emulate this model. Andhra Pradesh will also attempt to do so by setting up specialised education and R&D institutes as a joint effort between the Government and the private sector. The State can also facilitate the development of entrepreneurial start-ups by providing enabling mechanisms like venture capital.

Finally, the State will need to ensure that effective skill transfer takes place between the R&D laboratories, the educational institutes and the field/industry. This is a big challenge, especially in agriculture. To develop agriculture in rain-fed areas, for example, the State will need to focus not only on research to promote dryland agriculture but also on extension, that is, demonstrating the benefits of the improved technology and practices developed to persuade farmers to adopt them. In fact, a large part of China's agricultural productivity increases and agricultural growth have come from effective extension programmes.

> Andhra Pradesh will aim to become the 'Education Capital of India' by building 15 to 20 unique educational institutions in the State

• *Conducting focused and effective promotion:* Andhra Pradesh will have to compete for private investment not only with other states but also with other countries. Thus, active promotion is critical to attracting investment on the scale required. The State will need to design and conduct highly effective promotional campaigns. The goal should be nothing short of getting the best companies in every sector of focus to participate in Andhra Pradesh's growth programme. The promotion effort will need to have a twin focus: targeted campaigns and quality promotion.

1. Targeted campaigns: For each growth sector, the State needs to identify a target group of domestic and international investors it wants to attract to the State. It then has to design promotion campaigns to woo these investors and build a oneto-one relationship with them. The Prime Minister of Malaysia, for instance, went on a worldwide, high quality promotion blitz, targeting specific IT communities as well as key IT companies around the world to attract investment to the countryÆs Multimedia Super Corridor project. The Government could even set up specialised bodies to facilitate promotion. Japan's deliberation councils, for example, are formal institutions that facilitate communication between the private sector and the government. These councils, organised along functional or industry lines, provide a forum to exchange market trend and business-related information and to discuss and formulate industrial policies. They have played an important role in winning the support of the private sector.

2. *Quality promotion:* In general, business promotion efforts by the Government have lacked the focus and professionalism of campaigns by the governments of countries like China, Korea and Taiwan. Recognising the need to compete for investment, the State Government will need to pay particular attention to this aspect, for instance, by conducting market research on investors and even enlisting professional help, perhaps from public relations agencies.

This broad approach to creating the growth engines will be implemented through specific initiatives by industry and the Government.

TRANSFORMING GOVERNMENT

The success of the first two elements of the growth agenda, development through growth engines and developing Andhra Pradesh and its people, will hinge on support from the Government. Moreover, overall economic growth will be possible only if the Government becomes more efficient and accountable. The Government will therefore need to significantly change its current role, withdrawing from sectors that do not need its attention and focusing on those that need both its attention and resources.

Furthermore, achieving the levels of growth targeted will require investment on a scale far beyond the State Government's resources. In many sectors, therefore, growth will have to come mainly from private investment.

The Government will encourage the development of these sectors through private investment, and shift its focus to actively facilitating market-based growth. It will also shift its focus and resources to the development of human capital and infrastructure, retaining, however, its role as a major provider of services in these areas. The Government's role would then take on the following dimensions: achieve focus, i.e., where in the economy to intervene; improve capability, i.e., how best to intervene to enable development; improve interface with citizens, i.e., how best to make service providers responsive and accountable to the people.

To achieve these objectives, the Government will act in several ways: (1) refocus Government priorities and spending; (2) decentralise governance and make it participatory by involving the people in the governance of their State; (3) introduce æElectronic Government', i.e., use IT-based services to de-mystify procedures and improve the citizen-Government interface; (4) become a SMART (Simple, Moral, Accountable, Responsive, Transparent) Government by improving transparency and accountability and ensuring effective and responsive services; (5) build the administrationÆs capabilities and enhance policy making and performance; and (6) take a lead role in persuading the Central Government to initiate regulatory and other reform.

> The Government will need to shift its spending from unproductive areas towards achieving high priority developmental goals.

Refocus priorities and spending

Though much future investment in economic growth will come from the private sector, the Government will remain responsible for investment in some key areas, for example, basic education and primary healthcare; poverty eradication; social welfare; rural services; and select infrastructure (e.g., in less developed regions of the State).

To achieve the ambitious targets of the growth agenda, the Government will, therefore, need to shift its spending towards achieving high priority developmental goals. Areas of inefficiency, such as growing establishment costs and redundancies in Government employment, must be corrected. This will entail reducing administrative and other non-developmental expenditure such as support to unproductive public sector undertakings. In parallel, spending on important sectors, such as basic education, primary healthcare, food security, rural development, and infrastructure, must increase.

Decentralise government

The Government will ensure a greater focus on decentralised and responsive administration by local government and participation by the community. The State Government will enable this shift in power and responsibility by providing active technical, resource, and policy support to local governments. It will also continue to promote the Janmabhoomi initiative described in the section 'Scenario: Past and Present'. In addition, the Government will ensure that the management of services is decentralised by involving local users. This will be achieved with the help of community-based organisations such as School Committees, Vana Samrakshana Samitis, etc.

Introduce Electronic Government

The Government will use several mechanisms to enhance the quality of the services it provides and dramatically improve interaction between the people and Government departments. To this end, the Government will automate its services and create electronic networks at all points of contact between the people and the Government. This will provide quick and convenient access to Government departments for services, such as obtaining a ration card, or procedures, such as obtaining clearances for an industrial project. The Government aims to ultimately provide Andhra Pradesh residents with 'one-stop, non-stop' services, by making automated services available round-the-clock and providing 'information kiosks' to ensure access to these services for all.

> The Government of Andhra Pradesh is committed to becoming a simple, moral, accountable, responsive and transparent government.

Become a SMART Government

The Government of Andhra Pradesh is committed to becoming a simple, moral, accountable, responsive and transparent government. It will do so by simplifying and rationalising procedures, guaranteeing citizens' 'right to information' on all government activities except certain sensitive areas, and providing mechanisms to ensure transparency, responsiveness and accountability.

Realising that complex and time-consuming procedures are a

major obstacle to growth, the Government has resolved to review, rationalise and simplify procedures in key areas. This will include automating clearances, wherever possible; creating high quality information systems to expedite decision making on clearances; and empowering the bureaucracy to quickly provide clearances.

To improve responsiveness and accountability (and, thereby, the quality of services), the Government will adopt mechanisms used in other countries such as the 'Citizen Charter' adopted by Canada and the UK. Through these charters, government agencies in these countries undertake to provide services of a specified standard and pay penalties if the standards are not met. In the UK, 16 such charters have been framed covering services provided to different customers: for education services there is a 'Parents' Charter'; for healthcare services, there is a 'Patients' Charter', and so on. Each charter lays down guaranteed performance levels for each aspect of service and corresponding penalties for deficiencies in providing it. The State has already made a start by drafting charters for select departments and public undertakings.

In addition, the Government will need to provide more effective statutory mechanisms to ensure the integrity of government officials and protect citizens against wrongdoing.

Strengthen policy making and improve performance

A capable, performance-oriented administration is the cornerstone of improved governance. Such an administration can be created by building skills and instituting better reward and appraisal systems. Government officials will be given many opportunities to build their skills. The State Government has already set up the Dr. M. Channa Reddy Human Resource Development Institute of Andhra Pradesh to build the capabilities of its officials. In addition, current initiatives, such as specialisation in specific areas and deputation to other states and national and international organisations, will continue. Skills could also be built by inducting professional managers from the private sector as well as bringing in outside expertise in select areas and for specific projects, e.g., privatisation.

A performance orientation will be achieved through better reward and appraisal systems. Good performers will be identified and adequately rewarded. In addition, to enable better performance, officials could be provided with stable tenures, that is, they could be allowed to remain in a position for at least 3-5 years.

Take a lead role in initiating reform

As stated earlier, the development of the growth engines will require major reform in regulation and procedure. To successfully achieve this, the State Government will need to enlist the co-operation of the Centre, since much of the reform sought falls in areas either completely controlled by the Central Government or jointly controlled by the Centre and State Governments. For instance, telecommunications is completely controlled by the Centre, while highways are jointly controlled by the Centre and the State. Furthermore, some regulation on industry, such as the reservation of some industries for the small-scale sector, is also decided by the Centre. Therefore, relaxations sought, such as dereserving sectors like garments and leather products, can be granted only by the Centre.

In addition, some of the initiatives to achieve the vision for individual sectors call for changes in the funding or design of programmes sponsored by the Centre. For example, the funding and design of public employment schemes like the Jawahar Rojgar Yojana and the Employment Assurance Scheme are decided by the Centre. To achieve its vision, the State Government would need to have the freedom to modify the design of such programmes.

All this means that the Andhra Pradesh Government will have to actively negotiate with the Central Government to bring about the change needed. There are many ways the State could do this. One method could be to make Andhra Pradesh a test case for such reform as has been done with the Electronic Government initiative.

Section 3 lays out the approach to and initiatives for improving governance in the State. This section also explains the Government's approach to financing the implementation of Vision 2020.

RAISING THE RESOURCES

The question that comes to mind is how the strategy to achieve the vision will be financed, given the enormous pressures on the

State budget. However, where there is confidence in achieving a programme, it is always possible to generate programmebased finance. Andhra Pradesh has already demonstrated this by becoming the first state to secure a World Bank loan to a state rather than a sovereign government. The approach taken to securing investmentùaggressive targets, capability building and performance improvement, and making a strong case for why Andhra Pradesh deserves the moneyùwill ensure that it continues to attract investment.

This is not to say that the Government will depend only on investment from external sources. On the contrary, it will also pursue a number of initiatives to raise the resources required.

The approach taken to securing investment – aggressive targets, capability building and performance improvement, and making a strong case for why Andhra Pradesh deserves the moneyùwill ensure that it continues to attract investment.

First, the Government will need to prioritise its spending and consolidate its fiscal position. This will mean concentrating its resources on crucial areas such as poverty eradication, primary education and basic healthcare, and undertaking public sector reform. In addition, the Government will need to raise its capital budget.

Second, the Government will need to manage its expenditure better. Better maintenance of assets, completing ongoing projects before making fresh commitments, and selecting new projects and schemes on strict cost-benefit criteria will be major elements of this approach.

Third, the State needs to make its tax administration more efficient and maximise its revenue from tax collections. This will require a tax reform strategy that achieves systemic change as opposed to rate increases. The main elements of this strategy would be simplifying and rationalising the tax structure which today comprises several kinds of taxes; broadening the tax base; and using information technology for more effective tax administration.

Fourth, the Government will need to initiate growth-enhancing reforms in various sectors. The focus will be on inducing growth by ensuring the optimal utilisation of natural resources; enabling effective use of physical assets; and encouraging significant participation by the private sector by way of increased private investment.

In fact, since private investment will be key to achieving most of the growth targets, the Government will act on many fronts to attract this investment: boost infrastructure; reform policy and simplify procedures; help its labour force build its skills; ensure a focus on improving productivity in all sectors of the economy; and launch aggressive promotion campaigns aimed at domestic and foreign investors.

This strategy to finance the growth agenda is comprehensively discussed in the final chapter of this document, 'Raising the Resources'.

Countries achieving high levels of development in the last 30 years like Japan and Korea have done so through approaches that incorporate the components of Andhra Pradesh's growth agenda. Both Japan and Korea have undertaken development thrusts in select sectors of the economy. Japan focused on shipbuilding, synthetic fibres, electronics and steel; Korea focused on six sectors including steel, petrochemicals and machinery.

These countries have also built their capabilities in parallel. One of the priorities for the Ministry of Internal Trade and Industry (MITI), Japan's policy-making body, was to build infrastructure to enable industry. Korea invested heavily in primary and secondary education to build its people's skills and enable them to take advantage of opportunities created by economic policies. Both Korea and Japan acted to make their governments capable and strong. Korea explicitly recognised the need for capable bureaucrats and recruited qualified technocrats and academicians into government. Japan empowered its bureaucrats and insulated them from politics by creating an independent body to manage their appointment and compensation. While some aspects of their political and business systems need to change now to accommodate a more globalised economy, Andhra Pradesh can learn from their earlier successes9 . 9 Despite the recent economic crisis in

Indonesia, Thailand, Korea and Malaysia and the economic downturn in Japan, India can learn a great deal from the achievements of these countries. By emulating their successes (building world class companies, creating infrastructure which continues to be an asset, developing healthy, educated and skilled people, and creating tremendous opportunities for them), and avoiding pitfalls (excessive creation of unproductive assets; insufficient deregulation of financial institutions; and slowness in transforming into nimble, information-based economies), India can achieve similar levels of development.

Assam

Vision : 2025

Assam: Vision 2025

1. INTRODUCTION

1.1 Status & Potential

Last two decades of the 20th Century witnessed unprecedented changes in the history of human development. On the one hand the cyber revolution and the introduction of global networking in communication have made most parts of the world easily accessible. They have brought into being the concept of a 'global village' thereby throwing open enormous possibilities for each and every global citizen. Thus a global market has emerged for sharing the opportunities by all. On the other hand. The emergence of a consensus amongst most of the nations of the world, through the institution of the World Trade organisation, has brought into being a rule based trading system where one has to be competitive to survive. This consensus has not only set in a process of liberalisation but also knocked down the barriers of 'protectionism.' The emerging opportunities have come with consequent risks. Unless our economy is efficient and the products are competitive, the changes of success will be fast receding. Therefore, there is no escape from quick streamlining of our economy for efficient production and high growth by tapping the existing potentials.

1.1.2 Assam with a total area of 78438 sq.km., two major rivers with a number of perennial tributaries, 2.24 crore people and varieties of natural resources is a sleeping giant whose energy is yet to be tapped. The State which had once a promising economy, has today slided into poverty and backwardness. At the beginning of the post independence era, Assam was ranked among the prosperous States of the country. The per capita income in Assam in 1950-51 was 4% above the national average but as the time passed, it gradually came to the all India average level in 1954-55 and slipped down further in the following years. In 1996-97 it stood at Rs.1628 which was 41% below the all India average of Rs.2761. the growth rate of the Gross Domestic product (GDP) in Assam since 1987 has been declining. While the all India growth rate of GDP during the period 1987 to 1999 has been around 65%, in case of Assam it has been 3.7% in the beginning and has come down to 1.8% in 1998-99.

1.1.3 Not only that the GDP growth rate has been declining, the more disturbing factor has been the changes that have taken palace during the last 30 years in the sectoral composition of the state GDP in 1970-71, primary sector made only a contribution of 41.4% in 1996-97. The share of secondary sector during the same period came down from 14.5 to 12.1%. However the tertiary sector contribution went up from 31.3% to 46.5% during this period. The growth of tertiary sector has been apparently at the cost of the primary and the secondary sectors and substantially due to the increase in employment in the Government service. There is a continuous pressure for employment in the Government sector since very little opportunities exist in the private sector within the State. The State Government has limited resources to meet the demand for jobs by young men and women. The amount of resources spent on the Government employees leaves very little for investment that is needed for development of the primary sector of the economy. On the other hand, 45% of the rural population today lives below the poverty line and it is well nigh impossible to burden them with any further tax to generate resources. The message out of the situation is loud and clear. Rural economy has to be boosted at top priority and more income has to be generated for the 70% of the population which depends upon the primary sector activities. Opportunities of self-employment have to be created for gearing up the secondary sector and thus reduce the pressure on the Government for jobs. For both these purposes investment has to be arranged from all possible sources and that too in the shortest possible time.

1.1.4 Growing unemployment has been a serious cause of

concern. Around 9.85 lakh educated persons were registered with the various employment exchanges in the State in 1997. About 9.50% of these registered persons were graduates and 87.5% of them were matriculates and HSSLC holders. As these numbers swell over the coming years, avenues have to be created for providing them gainful employment. Farm sector holds the brightest promise to tackle this problem and massive efforts would be needed to create opportunities in this sector. IT sector is another area where job opportunities can be found in large number for educated unemployed and this has to be tapped to the maximum possible extent by gearing up suitable vocational/educational programmes in the early years of the next century.

1.1.5 While the economy has been sliding all these years, the population growth has been exceptionally high in the State. While the population in the country during the last three decades (1961-91) grew by 92.7%, it has grown by 107.4% in Assam during the same period. Population density in Assam was 286/sq.km as against the national average of 267/sq.km in 1991. The reasons for this unusual growth are well known. Overall result of this growth has been the breakdown of the State's economy. The population of the State is expected to reach around 4 crore by 2025 which would put tremendous pressure on land and infrastructure. Serious efforts are, therefore, required to rein in all factors, including migration of foreigners, which are contribution to this growth.

1.1.6 The infrastructure development in the State has been extremely slow. It has been lagging behind almost every State of the country except that of Orissa, Rajasthan, Madhya Pradesh, Himachal Pradesh , Jammu & Kashmir and other North Eastern States. Power generation and distribution is not adequate to support the growth of industry in the State. The conditions of roads and bridges are not at all conducive for promoting any worthwhile economic activity like tourism. These deficiencies in infrastructure have to be attended on priority if economic activities and services are to be supported and encouraged.

1.1.7 However, a silver lining in the dark clouds has been visible during this period of depressing economy. On the human resource development front, the State has fared rather well. The literacy rate, according to 54th round of National Sample survey, has been 80% against the all India average of 60%. This encourages us to hope for substantial avenues of employment in the job market outside the State. A well defined strategy to expose our young men and women to the requirements of the newly emerging job market within and outside the country is needed. The level of literacy among the women, Tribels and scheduled caste people has also been very encouraging and sustained efforts are needed to improve upon the same and to assist these educated persons in finding out a fruitful vocation for themselves. The literate women hold the key to population control and development of healthy and accomplished future generations. This potential has also to be exploited. To properly channelise the energies of youth, sports activities shall have to be encouraged and quality facilities for it would need to be developed.

1.1.8 The picture today in respect of foreign direct investment, setting up 100% export oriented units and establishment of new industries in the State is dismal and needs focussed attention urgently. The factor responsible for the stagnation in trade and commerce on one hand and lack of participation of private sector in the development activities on the other, is the sudden discontinuation of contacts with the East and South East Asian countries with whom there existed traditional links before independence. Tremendous potential for trade, commerce, tourism and investment can be created if these linkages are revived. Sustained efforts shall have to be made to attract investment for the economic and infrastructural development and to open up the economy of the state to reap the benefits in the changing global scenario.

1.1.9 Health infrastructure in the State needs development to improve the services for better quality of life of the people and the deficiencies require to be made up as early as possible. Special attention is needed for the health of children and women who hold the key for the future.

1.1.10 The existing rate of investment in the State can take its NSDP from Rs.15017 crores (1997-98) to Rs.41032 crores by the end of 2019-20 at constant prices of 1993-94. The per capita income may touch Rs.11496 mark by the same time if the current rate of growth of population continues, which would be below the projected National average of per capita income. A well defined strategy to bring the per capita income to the level of national average would need exceptionally high rate of about 8.6% for the growth of GDP. However the planning for next 25 years would have to be done to gradually achieve parity between state and the National average of per capita income and the GDP growth by 2025.

1.1.11 Uncertainty of planning process arising out of dwindling resources, mixed with its extensive coverage without any sharp focus on vital development sectors, has affected the progress over the last few decades and this needs correction. The focus of planning has to be shifted from expenditure oriented sprinkling exercise to a sector specific growth approach and to reduce all unproductive and avoidable investments. The deficits in budgeting have to be brought down to zero to endure full attainment of plan objectives. This can be done by augmentation of all available resources and encouraging private investments.

1.1.12 Above all, the most important factor for development is our attitude towards work. The despondency that we are backward and neglected, has become a cliche. This seems to have got so deeply ingrained in our collective conscience that we stopped all introduction for finding our own weaknesses. This fatalism must be shed lest we are overtaken by an impending tragedy. The experience, world over, has shown and also proved that hard work, discipline and foresight can achieve miracles. This must be our motto in the new century. Our commitment to international agreement relating to WTO and IPR makes it expedient on our part to be competitive and avoid seeking refuge under the past glory. Contour of State's pride and glory would have to be defined afresh in the next century in the light of the emerging situation. Hard work and zest for excellence alone can enable us to face the challenge and competition in the global economy of the new century.

1.2 Strategic Theme

1.2.1 The basic objective of the sectoral strategy to initiate a process of synchronised development between the existing government agencies in order to achieve a resurgent economy, which not only can withstand the sweeping process of 'liberalisation' and 'globalisation' but also improve the quality of life of every citizen in Assam. The main thrust area is the Rural Economy which provides livelihood for 70% of our population.

Rural economy encompasses Agriculture and allied sectors, small and medium industry, handloom and cottage industry and land reforms. It is obvious from the present trend that the flow of outside investment in these sectors will be marginal. Therefore, the Government proposes to adopt a direct intervention strategy to alleviate poverty and minimise unemployment. A major component of this intervention includes strategic development of 'human resource.' The available education infrastructure together with the existing literacy level will be further augmented for a break through. Running parallel to this will be increased investment in social sectors like health, nutrition, welfare activities including upliftment of the economically backward communities. The final objective will be to improve the quality of life for all in Assam.

1.2.2 The Vision : Assam 2025 envisages a partnership with the private sector to tap their resources and technology, particularly in the areas of power, communication, transport and industry. The existing resources available with the Government are far from adequate to establish the infrastructure for rapid industrial growth. Therefore, the sectoral strategy is specially designed to dovetail the private Sector capabilities into the economic growth process. The Government will play the role of a facilitator for augmenting private sector participation.

1.2.3 The sectoral strategy lays utmost emphasis on sectors like Tourism and Handloom where Assam traditionally enjoys comparative advantage. Our strength and potentials in these sectors have to be properly harnessed. Assam combined with the whole of North East, has enormous potential to became a tourist paradise. We have not been able to tap even a fraction of this potential to our advantage. Moreover, this smokeless industry can provide large number of direct and indirect employment even in the remotest part of the State. Similarly, our traditional handloom and handicraft products have been the envy of our competitors. We need to develop these products for higher value addition in the world market. It can open up new avenues for our traditional weavers and craftsmen. We need to maximise our gains in these sectors where we have the potentials. Thus the following sectoral strategy endeavours to lay down the blue print for an integrated economy to take on the challenges of coming 25 years.

2. RURAL ECONOMY

a. Increase the agriculture production in Assam and modernise agriculture operation.

b. Increase the production of spices and horticulture crops.

c. Improve and augment ideginous livestock population in order to increase Milk, Meat and Egg production.

d. Increase fish production to meet the 100% requirement of the state.

e. Increase production of Muga and Eri Silk for development of cottage silk industry.

f. Land reforms.

g. Increase employment opportunities with optimum resource utilisation in rural areas.

h. Initiate steps to patent the natural resources and products.

2.1 Agriculture

2.1.1 Objectives

- Rice production in the state shall be increased to 135 lakh M.T. by the end of 2025.
- Production of mustard and other oil seeds shall be increased to 7.5 lakh M.T. by the end of 2025.
- Wherever needed, facilities and incentives shall be introduced to encourage mechanisation of different farming operation in phased manner.
- Concerted efforts shall be made to increase the production of spices and horticulture crops to 5.2 lakh M.T. respectively.
- Effort would be made to increase the production of other crops in order to achieve self sufficiency.

2.1.2 Strategy

- For increasing the agricultural production, additional 10 lakh hectares of agriculture land would be provided with assured irrigation facilities by the end of 2003. Samridha

Krishak Yojna would continued to be implemented till that time.

- High yielding variety of seeds and fertilizers would be popularised among the farmers. Private enterprise would be encouraged to setup seed farms to produce HYV seeds for meeting the demand of the farmers.
- Flow of bank credit to the farmers would be augmented to meet their full requirement of loan in phased manner.
- Adequate marketing and storage facilities shall be provided to the farmers at affordable price and new markets for the local produce shall be located with stable link. Institutional finance support shall be ensured and community information centre network shall be ensured for making marketing and other information's available to the farmers.
- Cropping intensity would be increased to 177% from the present 146% by introducing farm mechanisation. Use of power-tillers and tractors on large scale would be encouraged through appropriate schemes.
- Special programme would be undertaken to produce ginger, black-pepper and turmeric. Processing of these spices and marketing of the same shall be arranged.
- Production of Banana and Pineapples would be increased by a special programme in identified areas and marketing & processing facilities would be developed to utilise this production.
- All these activities shall be organised through the Field Management committees (FMC).
- FMCs would be accorded legal status through appropriate legislation. Young farmers Development Agency (YFDA) would be set up in all districts on the pattern of FMC to motivate young people in developing agriculture as a commercial venture. Participating young men would be entitled to benefits of Social Security Scheme.

2.2 Veterinary

2.2.1 Objectives

- Production of Milk would be increased to 3000 Million Ltrs. By 2025.
- Production of Meat would be increased to 2.5 lakh M.T. by 2025.
- Production of Eggs would be increased to 3500 Millions by 2025.

2.2.2 Strategy

- Intensive programme for increasing the number of Milch cattle, Poultry, Pigs and Goats shall be under taken through the FMCs adjacent to the existing veterinary centres.
- Veterinary and Artificial Insemination services shall be made available to the FMCs.
- Processing and marketing facilities would be created through private enterprise.
- Technology Mission would be setup to improve the local indigenous breeds of animals.
- Intensive programme for fodder development would be launched to support the growing animal population. Fodder would be grown as part of Crop Rotation System and under forestry programmes.

2.3 Fishery

2.3.1 Objectives

Surplus production would be generated by 2025 beyond the local market demand of the state keeping the target of 22k.g. per capita consumption against the present consumption of 7.5k.g. per person.

2.3.2 Strategy

- "Operation Blue Revolution" would be launched by 2001 to increase fish production. In the first phase, production would be increased by 84000 MT by 2004 and the gap between the demand and supply would be brought down to 15% production would be increased to meet the expected demand of 7.72 lakh MT by 2025.

- All tanks, ponds and jheels in the state developed/created under programmes of various departments shall be listed through the FMCs and programme for fish-rearing shall be introduced in an intensive manner.
- Total ban would be imposed to capture brood and junvenile fish and for this purpose suitable training and extension programmes would be undertaken at each FMC level.
- Special programme for setting up of Fish Feed Outlets would be launched in each development block to meet the requirements of different ponds etc. of each block. Private sector would be entertained for this purpose on priority.
- Private sector would be encouraged in the field of marketing and development of cold storage and transport facilities.

2.4 Sericulture, Handloom and Textiles

2.4.1 Objectives

- Handloom sector would be developed as a competitive and commercial industry by upgrading technology and capacity, preserving the cultural heritage of the state linked with this industry.
- Industry would be made customer focussed and quality driven.
- Export market would be located for the indigenous product and marketing would be facilitated.
- Sualkuchi would be declared as a Handloom heritage Village to preserve the designs and the textile traditions of Assam and to provide facilities for training to the weavers.

2.4.2 Strategy

- Additional areas will be brought under Som and Era plantation for increasing the production of Muga and Eri Silk.

- Six lakhs weavers would be added to the commercial fold by 2005.
- The potential in tune with market requirements would be provided to entrepreneurs and co-operatives.
- An Export promotion Cell under the Assam Government Marketing Corporation shall be crated to study the markets, make fashion forecast, produce marketable design, facilitate buyer-seller contacts.
- A permanent Exhibition Centre would be developed at Guwahati and a sale-cum-display counter shall be opened at Bombay for the products of rural artisans.
- Use of community information centres shall be made for providing market information to the weavers.
- Exiting department production centres shall be opened up for participation by private sector for quality improvement and better marketing.
- Looms of six lakh weavers shall be upgraded by 2005 through suitable R & D intervention.
- The domestic weavers would be provided training, raw material and technological inputs to improve their skills and consequent induction to commercial weavers' group.

2.5 Land Reforms

2.5.1 Objectives

- More land would be made available for agricultural and forestry purposes.
- Legal rights would be given to the farmers in respect of their lands.

2.5.2 Strategy

- Land reforms would be implemented vigorously and all cases under ceiling laws etc. would be disposed off by 2005. The surplus land so acquired shall be distributed among the landless farmers.

- Assam Tenancy Act 1971 shall be implemented more vigourously to protect the rights of the tenants.
- Annual pattas in the rural areas would be converted into periodic patta to enable the farmers to avail loans etc. from the financial institutions . While doing so special care would be exercised to ensure that the illegal migrants and foreigners do not acquire rights over the land.
- The process of land consolidation would be pursued to enable the farmers reap the full benefits of assured irrigation and farm mechanisation.
- Special drive would be undertaken to provide legal right documents to the tribal farmers in the tribal areas.

3. ECONOMY & OTHER SECTORS

a. Encourage new private ventures for the development of industries in the State in accordance with the policy of the Central Government for the North East and the policy of the State.

b. Special emphasis on promoting the IT industry through the private sector.

c. Develop Food processing based on banana, pineapple, and spices.

d. Promote Industry based on the product of Gas Cracker Project.

e. Develop Tourism in a sustained way without any adverse impact on the natural and cultural heritage of the State.

f. Organize Small Scale Industries in the rural areas.

g. Initiate Steps for developing Trans-Border trade with the neighbouring countries of East and South East Asia.

3.1 Major Industries

3.1.1 Objectives

- Potential of the New Industrial Policy 1999 announced by the Govt. of India has to be tapped and private entrepreneurs need to be attracted to the State for setting up industries.

- The opportunities offered by the Software park, at Guwahati, Proposed Gas Cracker project at Lepetkota and the increased production of Oil seeds, banana, pineapples and spices in the agricultural sector have to be tapped.

3.1.2 Strategy

- Procedures for issue of licenses etc. wherever needed, allotment of land industrial sheds etc. would be simplified.
- Every district shall have a growth centre by 2005. Deputy Commissioners would be made responsible for speedy clearance of all proposals for setting up industries within their respective jurisdiction and powers for this purpose would be decentralised.
- Electric power connection would be provided to the intending investors by the Deputy Commissioner for setting up the industry and powers for this purpose also would be given to the Deputy Commissioners.
- Five more Science Technology Parks would be set up in the State by 2010.
- In each of the DCs office a cell called 'Jeevika Sahayika shall be opened by March 2001. This cell would provide guidance for self-employment and assist the entrepreneurs in all maters for setting up their unit and also provide them guidance on marketing, etc.

3.2 Small Scale & Cottage Industries

3.2.1 Objectives

- Small Scale and cottage industries based on the local resources would be developed to provide additional employment and income to a large number of people living in rural and urban areas.

3.2.2 Strategy

- Districts level set up for the development of SSI/ Cottage

Industries would be reinforced and activated.

- New skills that may be required for utilisation of the local resources would be developed among the people.
- Guidance on marketing, design development etc. would also be provided through "Jeevika Sahayika" Cell in the DCs office.

3.3 Tourism

3.3.1 Objectives

- By the end of 2025 business turn over worth Rs.136000/- crores would be generated providing employment to 10.13 lakhs persons in the State.
- By the end of year 2020, twenty one lakhs domestic tourists and 20000 foreign tourists would be attracted to the State. This target would be increased to 27 lakh domestic tourists and 30000 foreign tourists by 2025.

3.3.2 Strategy

- Private investment would be encouraged in the tourism sector and special incentive packages, including allotment of land at concessional rates shall be offered for development of tourist facilities.
- Tourism packages shall be diversified to include golf tourism, eco tourism, tea tourism in association with private sector.
- Community information centre network would be used for tourist information.
- Road, power and communication infrastructure shall be developed for the identified tourist destinations.
- Co-operation among the North Eastern States in developing a suitable tourist package involving cultural and natural heritage sports in all the states would be sought. Efforts would be made to attract tourists for the entire North East as a combined effort of all states to offer variety to the visiting tourists.

- Places of historical and cultural importance in the State would be identified and declared as heritage sites and a special plan would be undertaken to develop these sites by the end of 2010 in phased manner.
- Joint efforts along with the Railways and civil Aviation authorities would be made to improve the facilities at major stations and airports of tourist importance.
- A co-ordinated approach would be put in place between the departments of forest, environments, culture and police to facilitate safe tourism.
- Facilities for training of young girls and boys for working as tourist Guides and other tourism related courses shall be developed in the private and Government institution.
- Govt. of India would be requested to relax further restrictions on the movement of foreign tourists in the entire North Eastern region and aggressive promotion campaign abroad would be undertaken with the help of Govt. of India agencies.
- To utilise the Golf courses in the State presently owned by the Tea Gardens and oil Companies for the purpose of development of tourism, dialogue with the owners of such Golf courses shall be initiated and a suitable scheme would be evolved.
- Steps would be taken by the Govt. to encourage private investment for opening sale counters of locally made handicrafts, handloom and textiles, silk products etc. at different tourist locations and quality control and price control would be effected strictly for the benefit of the tourists.
- A Cultural Village at Buraphar near Kaziranga would be developed as a tourist resort through private sector.

4. INFRASTRUCTURE

a. Improve rural roads and bridges vital for the marketing of agriculture products and transport of agriculture inputs.

b. Develop urban roads/States highways and National highways for the development of tourism, trade and commerce.

c. Increase power generation to sustain industrial and agricultural growth.

d. Develop a new planned city near Guwahati to decongest the existing city.

e. Maintenance and repairs of embankments to protect agricultural lands from the damaging effects of flood.

f. Develop facilities and amenities relating to railways, airlines, telephones and post and telegraph services in specified areas for the benefit of tourists.

g. Develop Inland Water Transport as an alternative means of transport of heavy cargo and as tourist attraction.

4.1 Roads and Bridges

4.1.1 Objectives

- The roads in the rural areas which cater to the needs of transportation of agriculture inputs and the agriculture produce need to be developed to facilitate growth of agriculture.
- To improve communication between the district and sub-divisional headquarters and to the tourist destinations, other state roads need to be developed.
- Important roads leading to the interior areas predominantly inhabited by SC and ST shall be developed.

4.1.2 Strategy

- 'Operation Blacktop' would be launched to improve all the roads connecting the districts and sub-divisional headquarters and the tourist destinations within 2007.

- A phased programme would be prepared by 15th August 2001 for this operation and funds will be mobilised to start the work.
- A phased programme for development of rural roads which are of importance for promoting agriculture growth, shall be prepare by 15th August 2001 and resources would be mobilised to execute the plan within 2010.
- To further facilitate communications across the river Brahmaputra a bridge between Jorhat and North Lakhimpur via Majuli would be provided. Similarly, between the twin cities of Guwahati two more bridges would be constructed to facilitate passenger and goods movement.
- Road Development Fund for improvement of urban roads and for rural roads would be set up by amalgamating resources under various programmes of the States Govt. and the Central Govt. for the purpose.
- Private investment would be entertained for the development of roads and suitable incentives would be offered to them.
- Government of India would be approached for the development of East-West Highways connecting Guwahati with the Still Well Road along the North and South Banks of the River Brahmaputra for the development of Trans-border trade. Similar highway shall be developed along the banks of River Barak.

4.2 Power Generation

4.2.1 Objectives

- To sustain the tempo of industrial and agricultural growth adequate power supply has to be made and generation has to be stepped up from the present 500 MW to 4360 MW by 2025.

4.2.2 Strategy

- Power generation in the state would be increased in phased manner.

- Special drive would be undertaken to provide electric connections to farmers in rural areas for encouraging farm mechnisation.
- To improve revenues, steps will be taken to bill the rural farmers suitably and meters will be provided to them.
- Independent power producers would be encouraged to participate in the power generation programme, especially for mini hydel project development.
- Reforms in power sector would be introduced in a phased manner according to the new power policy of the State.

4.3 Communications

4.3.1 Objectives

- To facilitate growth of tourism, industry, commerce and trade the telephone, railways, airlines, inland water transport and post and telegraph services have to be augmented and improved.
- Facilities and amenities in these sectors for specific locations of tourism and commercial importance will have to be augmented to the level of national standards.

4.3.2 Strategy

- A prospective plan would be prepared for developing and improving the services of railways, post and telegraphs and telephones for various tourist destinations and commerce and trade centres by 2001.
- Efforts would be made to provide double track on important sections of the railways and electrification of the tracks for improving the railways services at the earliest.
- Telephones and telegraph services would be expanded and optical fibre networking shall be put in place in the State in phased manner in the shortest possible time.
- International airlines would be approached to start new flights to and for Guwahati or touch Guwahati by their existing flights to cater to the needs of tourists and businessmen.

- Private investment would be encouraged in developing road transport and buses with high standard amenities for tourists shall be inducted in the State.
- Night navigation facilities in national waterways No.1 would be developed by 2005 and utilised for cargo transportation as well as for tourism promotion.

4.4 Other Infrastructure

4.4.1 Objectives

- The Major cities and town where congestion is increasing, need to be decongested in a planned way.
- Residential, educational and recreational facilities in the capital city and in other important towns shall be improved and augmented to cater to be future needs.

4.4.2 Strategy

- A prospective plan for developing the infrastructure for water supply, electricity, waste disposal and drainage shall be prepared by the end of 2001 for the district headquarter towns of the State.
- The prospective plan would be implemented in a phased manner by the end of 2010.
- A twin city of Guwahati would be developed on the north bank of river Brahmaputra to accommodate 20 lakh people by the end of 2025. The development of this city would be undertaken in a phased manner.
- To decongest the existing city of Guwahati certain commercial establishments would be shifted out of the city and accommodated in identified locations for the purpose in the new city.
- Sattelite towns around Guwahati and other existing towns shall be developed according to the needs in a phased manner with the help of private investment to provide important service facilities for neighbouring villages.
- For public convenience all district offices of Kamrup

district would be brought under multi stories office complex by 2005.

4.5 Flood Control

4.5.1 Objectives

- Protection to agricultural lands and important infrastructure from the flood damages would be provided.

4.5.2 Strategy

- Master plan for flood control, prepared by the Brahmaputra Board shall be implemented in a phased manner.
- Co-operation of neighbouring states in implementing the plan for flood protection and prevention would be sought at the highest level.

5. HUMAN RESOURCE

a. Develop facilities for education in newly emerging disciplines.

b. Improve the existing facilities of education.

c. Encourage and promote sports for achieving excellence at national and international level.

d. Provide better health services to the people.

e. Provide clean and healthy natural environment to the people.

f. Check population growth, including prevention of illegal migration.

5.1 Education

5.1.1 Objectives

- Education for all up to elementary level would be available by 2010.
- 100% access and retention of students up to elementary stage with 0% drop out would be achieved by 2020.

- Steps shall be initiated for the improvement of quality of teachers.
- Upgradation of textbooks with emphasis on English and Mathematics would be carried out.
- Educational facilities for floating population in urban areas and reverine areas would be organised
- Universalisation of Higher Secondary Education would be achieved by 2020.
- Computer Education from class X to XII in all provincialised High & Higher Secondary schools would be arranged by 2005 and coverage of students of class VI to X under computer education progaramme would be completed by 2010.
- Facilities for specialised education in new emerging disciplines shall be developed.

5.1.2 Strategy

- 'Operation Talent' would be launched by 2001 to identify, train and employ the talented youth at different levels in different streams of studies. Promising students at different levels from the state would be picked up and provided support in pursuing further higher studies and training. They would also be encouraged to take up research work which may benefit the state economy.
- Expansion and extension of existing facilities and infrastructure in order to accommodate additional 11.7 lakh children in LP level and 5.3 lakh children in new upper primary level would be made.
- The DPEP programme at LP level would be extended beyond 2003 and to cover the 14 districts which are at present not covered.
- Teachers training programme under DPEP would be supplemented with the special effort of SCERT and NGOs would also be involved in training of teachers to achieve the targets by 2005.
- Computer Education facilities would be provided in schools

and for teachers training in a phased manner.

- Various reforms in the schooling system would be effected in a phased manner.
- Institutes for information Technology and Indian Institute of Management would be set up in the State by the end of 2005 and 2007 respectively.
- Private investment would be encouraged in development of institutions offering professional and technical courses.
- Existing institutes and vocational centres would be upgraded to provide improved skills in old trades and new skills in emerging trades and subjects keeping in mind the need of various development sectors of the economy.

5.2 Health

5.2.1 Objectives

- Infrastructure for health services in the rural and urban areas would be completed within a short time.
- Immunisation to all children and women would be provided.
- Private sector and NGOs would be involved in extension of health services.
- Population shall be stabilised and net reproductive rate of 1.0 by would be achieved.
- Supply of safe drinking water and strict enforcement of Prevention of Food Adulteration Act would be ensured.
- Indian system of Medicine including production of herbs in the State would be encouraged.

5.2.2 Strategy

- The rural areas will be covered as per the norms under the health services through PHCs, CHCs and Sub-Centres. The entire infrastructure of these institutions would be completed by 2005 in phased manner.
- Incentive scheme for medical graduates and ayurvedic graduates to set up their own clinics/nursing homes/ mother and child care units in the rural areas would be

announced by 2001.

- Special annual drive would be undertaken to immunise the entire child population and women for safe motherhood.
- Family planning facilities would be made available at the door steps to all the married couples.
- Special efforts will be made to control and treat Malaria, TB, AIDS, Leprosy and Cataract.
- Private institution and NGOs would be encouraged to provide health services in the urban and rural areas and for their effective regulation appropriate law and rules would be framed which would be investor friendly as well as capable of protecting the interest of the patients.
- Progeny gardens shall be set up under the Forest Department/Agriculture Department/Private Sector for encouraging cultivation of medicinal plants for commercial purposes.

5.3 Sports & Youths Activities

- Existing facilities for sports in the State shall be upgraded in a phased manner.
- Facilities of national / international standard for swimming, flying, golfing and gymnastics shall be developed in a phased manner.
- Stadia in the rural areas shall be improved and properly equipped and suitably identified Stadia shall be upgraded to the national standards.
- 'Operation Talent' shall be launched to locate, train and employ the sports talent among young boys and girls.

5.4 Environment

- Planning of one lakh hectares of forest land would be undertaken with the help of NGOs and local community in a phased manner.
- 0.2 lakh hectares land area would be brought under rehabilitation of orchids, medicinal plants and non wood forest produce.

- Integrated eco-development programme would cover 1500 villages to reduce the dependence of the villagers on the forests.
- Bio-diversity conservation drive would be undertaken under protected areas network covering 500 villages on their fringes for socio economic development.
- Special programme will be initiated for fodder development through plantation on private lands.
- Anti pollution Laws, waste management laws would be strictly enforced.

5.5 Science and Technology

- Non conventional sources of energy would be popularised through a special drive to protect and preserve the natural forests.
- Research oriented work in the Universities and Colleges and other institutions in the State would be encouraged to evolve appropriate technologies for faster growth of agriculture and utilisation of local resources for industrial production.
- 'Operation Talent' would be launched to locate local talent, develop it and employ for the benefit of the State's economy.
- A 'Technological Museum' would be set up to preserve old machines equipments and designs etc, used in Assam in the past and which have now become or would be becoming obsolete.
- Programme for setting up Community information Centres all over the State shall expeditiously implemented.

6. WELFARE

a. Protect and preserve the cultural identity and traditions of different ethnic groups in the State.

b. Special attention for the orphans, disabled and other handicapped persons.

c. Special programme for helping the children, women, SC, ST, OBC, Tea and Ex-Tea garden people an minorities.

6.1 Strategy

- The existing programmes for the welfare of different ethnic groups of people shall be further strengthened in content and coverage.
- New initiatives would be started for meeting special needs of the underprivileged groups of people.
- Steps would be initiated for protection of cultural heritage and promotion of Art & Culture.
- Satriya dance would be patronised for bringing about qualitative improvement and recognition as major Indian Classical dance.
- Various indigenous rare art forms, literary writings, folk dances and songs etc. shall be appropriately documented and preserved in a museum.
- Institution like Jyoti Bharati and Srimanta Sankar Deva Kalakshetra would be supported for research and development of various aspects of art and culture of the State.
- Jyoti Chitraban would be developed to provide all morden facilities for production of quality films and training of personnels associated with the film industry
- To popularise films industry.
- To popularise films produced by the local artists/producers, chain of Mini cinema Halls shall be encouraged in the State through private investment.
- Autonomous councils in the tribal areas would be developed as an effective instrument of development of the tribal communities of the State.
- Special incentive schemes to encourage literacy among the girls would be undertake. Special incentives will also be offered to the girl students of poor families under the 'Operation Talent' to encourage entry into new vocations.

- Pre-primary classes shall be organised in every L.P.School to provide care for the infants.
- Voluntary agencies would be encouraged in the field of development of disabled children, orphans, old age persons, metally sick persons and other disadvantaged sections of the society.
- Activities under Rural Development programme would be targeted specifically for the underprivileged group of people and a suitable policy shall be adopted for providing better housing facilities in the rural areas.
- Solar energy would be utilised for providing household electricity in the remote tribal areas and char areas.

7. CONCLUSION

7.1 *Vision :* Assam 2025 envisages resurgent economy of the State, which will be capable of achieving higher growth. The rural sector remains at the centre piece of the blue print as the main thrust area, and its rapid development would be the top most priority for the Government. The vision strategy assumes that development of rural economy will have a cascading effect on other sectors. Allied sector like infrastructure, transport communication, power etc. will be able to attract private investments whereas the rural sector would require direct government intervention for rapid growth. Special emphasis has to be given to the development of human resource of the State. Over the last 50 years, although the Government has made considerable investment in the social sectors, there has not been appreciable harnessing of these investments. The vision document envisages to take full advantage of the investments already made by introducing systematic development of skill and knowledge of the work force as an integral part of human resource development programme.

7.2 The second important goal of Vision : Assam 2025 is to bring about a synchronisation amongst the various sectors of economy through this blue print of development so that duplication of effort and resources can be eliminated. Moreover, such synchronisation will generate greater development thrust through timely action on the part of various Government agencies. It will not only result in greater productivity, but also will help to achieve the set goals without endlessly increasing the size of Government organisations. The document thus envisages strict fiscal discipline and economy in Government expenditure so that increasing dependence on borrowing is slowly brought down.

7.3 Finally, one of the most important objectives of the Vision : Assam 2025 is to generate a synergy between the Government and the private sectors. The hitherto existing untapped capital and human resource of private sector need to be dovetailed into Government of the State economy. Thus the Government will assume the role of a facilitator to help the private sectors grow to their optimum level. That will help in generation of employment without involving expenditure from State exchequer. It will further create avenues for downsizing government and at the same time help in tackling the menacing problem of unemployment. Thus the State economy can be put on a path of sustainable growth through a vibrant partnership between government and private sectors.

Chhattisgarh

Vision : 2010

Chhattisgarh : Vision 2010

Chhattisgarh: Competitive analysis

Before embarking on a Visioning exercise it is important to assess the State's potential in terms of its inherent strengths and weaknesses. The SWOT analysis presented herein (Exhibit II.1) is not intended to be exhaustive. However, it is indicative of some of the primary issues that the State will need to contend with, going forward.

Exhibit II.1

Strengths	Opportunities
• Rich mineral and natural resources • Surplus power • Low land cost • Favourable industrial climate • Fiscal position	• 'New State' advantage • Energy deficit in the country • Location - Logistic hub • Services Industry • Partnerships
• Landlocked and limited local markets • Vulnerability to drought • Poor communication and physical infrastructure • Non-availability of skilled manpower	• Over dependence on natural resources could lead to lop-sided development • Suspicion & opposition to change in minds of the people • Short term political compulsions
Weaknesses	**Threats**

WEAKNESSES

- **Landlocked and limited local markets**

  As a virtually landlocked area, the State has to depend heavily on its road and railway network, which is to a considerable extent limited. Additionally a large rural population coupled with low per capita income limits the size of the local market. However, a few cities in the State have demonstrated the potential to develop into substantial local markets, as is evident from their current levels of per capita spending.

- **Low telephone density**

  The telephone density of approximately 1 in the State is low compared to the national average. This particularly inhibits the efficient functioning of the service industry that depends heavily on Information and Communication Technology (ICTs).

> The absence of large local markets, skilled labour and adequate physical infrastructure are some of the key weaknesses of the State.

- **Low skilled labour**

  The relatively low level of industrialisation in the State has limited the development of skilled labour. The current availability of skilled labour is further restricted to select industries only due to the absence of a divergent industrial base.

- **Limited physical infrastructure**

  The State still has vast areas of undeveloped land and some regions that have been untouched by modern development. While this is the result of years of prior neglect in developing proper physical infrastructure it now constitutes the weakest link in the progress towards economic development.

- **Frequent droughts**

  Although the average rainfall in Chhattisgarh compares well with several other states, neglect of traditional water preservation practices in recent times has led to frequent droughts. Further, the proportion of irrigated area in the State is only 16 percent of the total cultivable area. There is however, potential to raise the proportion of irrigated area to 75 percent of the total cultivable area.

- **Low urbanisation**

  The State ranks low on urbanisation index with limited number of urban centres, which are confined to central Chhattisgarh. Low urbanisation and lack of adequate physical infrastructure are the key reasons why Chhattisgarh is low on national perception, and also ranks low on development indicators along with the perceived potential for development.

> Low urbanisation and lack of adequate physical infrastructure are the key reasons why Chhattisgarh ranks low on national perception.

THREATS

- **Over dependence on natural resources**

  The State must take care to use its natural resources judiciously. An emphasis on balanced and all-round development would be essential to ensure environmentally sustainable growth. Having said that, there is little doubt that the optimal utilisation of natural assets holds the key to State's development process.

- **Political compulsions**

  Political will at all levels is a must to enable any kind of change. Any disruption in the pace or direction of proposed reforms could hamper the swift movement towards economic development.

- **Suspicion of and opposition to change**

  The people of the newly formed State being accustomed to prior neglect, may look upon any kind of change with doubt or suspicion. The State must, in the spirit of participatory democracy, take steps to build consensus and infuse a sense of confidence in its people with specific reference to the objectives, direction and pace of economic development

While it is absolutely essential to understand the weaknesses and threats (significant but not exhaustive), it is the aggregate of strengths and opportunities that infuses the State and its people with a sense of optimism about the future.

STRENGTHS

- **Rich natural resources**

  Undoubtedly the biggest strength of the State, Chhattisgarh used to contribute 46% of mineral revenues to undivided Madhya Pradesh and is ranked second in the list of mineral producing States in the country. It has rich deposits of limestone, iron-ore, copper-ore, rock phosphate, manganese ore, bauxite, coal, asbestos and mica. In fact Chhattisgarh, along with Orissa and Jharkhand constitute over 80% of the nation's coal reserves. Chhattisgarh also has proven reserves of diamond – which can, in the future, be a large source of income for the State.

  Although the State already has a substantial presence of core industries, a large part of the mineral potential is yet untapped, providing Chhattisgarh with a unique opportunity to use its mineral wealth to spur economic development. Apart from minerals, Chhattisgarh also possesses a large forest cover encompassing approximately 44% of the total geographical area. However, the true potential of the minor forest produce is yet to be assessed and utilised. The State has abundant but untapped water resources – essential for harvesting the potential of agriculture.

- **Surplus power**

  Chhattisgarh is fortunate to be one of the few States that are currently power surplus. This could be an important criteria for Industrialists making project and investment decisions, to Chhattisgarh's advantage. Presence of low grade coal makes Chhattisgarh an ideal location for setting up of low cost pit head based thermal power plant, capable of generating power to meet the requirements of other States.

- **Favourable labour climate**

  Though the relative skill base is low, the presence of a large number of willing and able-bodied people contributes to the presence of a substantial workforce. The State has a high worker participation rate (male and female) and a high labour force in the 15-39 age group. It also has one of the lowest losses in person-days in the country attributed to labour problems.

> Apart from minerals, Chhattisgarh also possesses a large forest cover encompassing approximately 44% of the total geographical area. However, the true potential of the minor forcst produce is yet to be assessed and utilised.

- **Relatively low land cost**

  With a lower population density and urbanisation ratio, the State would be able to offer land at extremely competitive prices for some time to come.

- **Fiscal position**

  The fiscal deficit situation of the State is currently under control. It also has reliable sources of public finance and possesses no deficit on account of either the State Electricity Board or Road Transport Corporation. This is contrary to the situation in other states, wherein these agencies are the principal contributors to the fiscal deficit.

- **Political Leadership and Bureaucracy**

  The number of bureaucrats and government employees compared to the other States in the country. This has also resulted in one of the lowest expenditures in the country on government functioning. The presence of a strong, committed and focussed leadership is an asset.

OPPORTUNITIES

- **'New State' advantage**

  The fulfillment of the demand for a separate State has given a new sense of identity and pride to the local people. Being a new State and with limited legacies of the past, this is a historic opportunity for Chhattisgarh. It can leverage on this status to undertake reforms and frame policies to aid rapid social and economic development. No past legacies provide the State with an opportunity to prepare policies which are based on contemporary economic principles and which help create responsive governance.

- **Locational advantage**

  The geographic location of the State is strategic – it borders seven states in the country. NH-6, which connects the west to the east, passes through some of the most industrialised areas of the State. Chhattisgarh could use this geographic locational to its advantage to develop a logistics and warehousing network to service the region.

- **Demand for Energy in the country**

  While the rest of India faces acute power shortages, the same is not true of Chhattisgarh. Further, in view of the presence of large coal reserves in the State and the fact that it is situated in the middle of the national power grid makes it an ideal location for setting-up coal pit-head based thermal power plants.

- **Partnership**

  The State recognises the opportunity of an increasingly borderless world and the resulting benefits of forging partnerships with national and international communities, private and developmental institutions to spur economic development.

> By exploiting its unique locational position along with large coal reserves, Chhattisgarh has the potential to become the power generating hub of India.

- **Value addition**

  Currently a large part of exports from the State is in form of raw material (across minerals, agriculture and forest produce). The state could capitalise on the abundant availability of basic raw material to encourage setting up of processing units for ensuring value addition and subsequently increasing avenues for employment and enhanced income.

- **Service industry**

  India has made rapid strides in the service industry in the past few decades. The State could potentially capitalise on these areas of country advantage, specifically in the field of information and biotechnology.

It is precisely this aggregate of strengths and opportunities that gives the State a positive and optimistic outlook on the future and the confidence to draft its Vision Statement.

THE VISION

Chhattisharh is richly endowed with natural resources. As a newly formed state and with the newly acquired independence to govern itself, the State is well poised to harness this natural advantage for the benefit of its citizens.

The natural optimism with which the State views its future is captured in the Vision Statement articulated by the Chief Minister of Chhattisgarh, Shri. Ajit Jogi:

"In the next 10 years we see the State of Chhattisgarh leveraging its 'new state' advantage in taking its rightful position amongst the fastest growing states in our country, where distress migration is a thing of the past, where it has a large service sector growth coupled with rapid increases in agriculture productivity leading to prosperity of our people, where all our people are, out of choice, gainfully employed and have the same (if not better) quality of life as some of the more economically advanced states in our country today ... where our factors of production (and goods and services) participate and compete more effectively in the new global economic environment ... more importantly, we see a State and its people empowered with the options to choose their own destiny, with specific reference to their way of life and greater interaction and integration with other states and peoples of the world ... to do this, Chhattisgarh must, over the next 10 years, seek to resolve the paradox of being a richly endowed state inhabited by poor people ..."

To realise this ambitious yet attainable vision, we have set for ourselves specific goals and priorities (Exhibit III.1 – overleaf):

Goal # 1 : Unlocking the value of our natural assets

Goal # 2 : Initiating the process of building world class physical infrastructure

Goal # 3 : Investing in the most precious resource of all – our human capital

> The State recognises this historic opportunity and the immense responsibility along with the challenges it faces in ensuring balanced economic and social development. However, it is equally keen and determined to begin the transformation of the State's fortunes.

Exhibit III.1

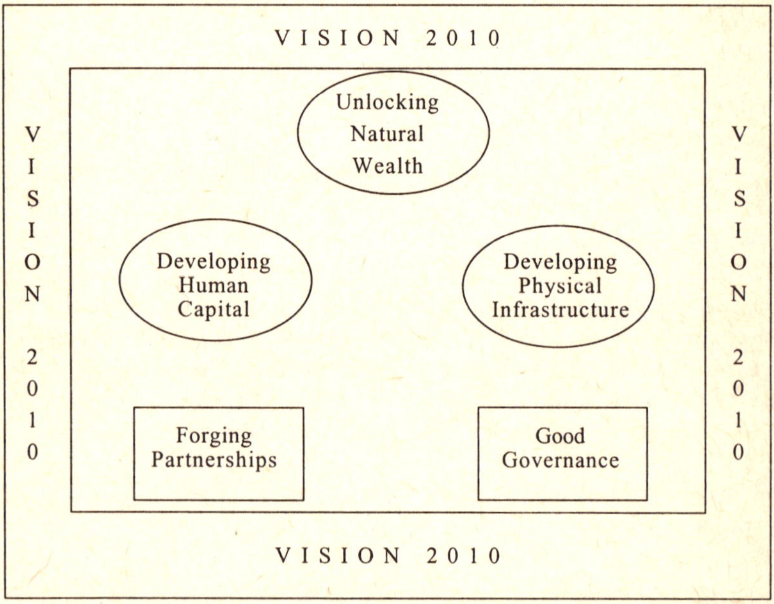

We recognise that these goals are not automatically attainable. Specific initiatives will have to be taken by the State to break the vicious cycle that has hitherto hampered social and economic progress. These include:

Initiative # 1 : Strengthening and adhering to the principles of good governance in terms of complete transparency, efficiency and accountability.

Initiative # 2 : Forging partnerships with national and international agencies for a best practice led approach to socio-economic development.

Finally, we believe that the combination of our goals and priorities along with the underlying strategic initiatives will, over the next 10 years, build the foundations of a more vibrant and modern economy that will set the pace of socioeconomic development for subsequent decades.

> The State would undertake two specific initiatives to break the vicious cycle hampering social and economic progress viz. strengthening and adhering to the principles of good governance and forging partnerships with national and international agencies.

SETTING MEASURABLE TARGETS— THE WAY FORWARD

The State realises that the Vision should be goal and target oriented and that these development objectives should be time bound and subject to scrutiny by a transparent monitoring mechanism. In order to realise the vision, the State has set for itself time bound goals with measurable targets that are discussed below:

Achieving 100% literacy - During the last decade, the State has made big strides in this area with total literacy increasing from 42.91% in 1991 to 65.18% in 2001 (Exhibit IV.1). The level of male literacy in Chhattisgarh today is better than the national average. Given the significance of education for overall social and economic development, the State would achieve 100% literacy by 2010 with a renewed focus on higher (and technical) education. Primary education would be made compulsory for all children till the age of 14 years.

Exhibit IV.1

Literacy Rate

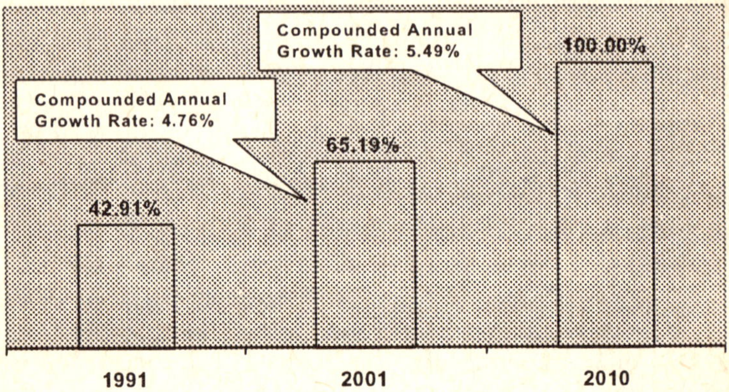

Shift in cropping pattern and double cropping - The State currently has an area of approximately 0.82 million hectares, which is under double cropping (representing only 17% of the total net cropped area). By 2010, 100% of the total netcropped area would be made suitable for double cropping.

Achieving 200 percent increase in the irrigation potential - The State currently has an irrigated potential of approximately 1.34 million hectares and would increase this irrigated potential to 4.02 million hectares by 2010, by increasing the number of water pumps across the State.

Ensuring 100 percent safe drinking water for all - The State currently has 54,816 hamlets, of which approximately 85% have access to drinking water. This existing coverage would be extended to all hamlets resulting in access to safe drinking water for all before 2010.

> The State realises that the Vision should be goal and target oriented and that these development objectives should be time bound and subject to scrutiny by a transparent monitoring mechanism.

Connecting all villages with metalled roads - As on date, metalled roads cover approximately 40% of the 19,720 villages in the State. By the year 2010 all weather roads would connect every village in the State.

Establishing rule of law - The State would ensure that there is an adequate law enforcing machinery in place and that citizens are made aware and responsible, to promote a civilised and just society. Along with the rights that every citizen enjoys in a democratic setup, the duties towards society would be highlighted so as to establish the supremacy of law above all.

Empowering women - Women in Chhattisgarh have traditionally enjoyed freedom denied to women elsewhere in the country. Ensuring reservations for women in local selfgovernance would further strengthen this position of women in Chhattisgarh.

Reducing poverty - Poverty reduction would be one of the priorities of the government. At present 38.91% of the State's population is below the poverty line. The government would work towards halving this number by 2010.

Access to health care for all - The ratio of number of hospital beds to total population in Chhattisgarh is 1:3316, which would be increased to 1:800. The State would also ensure the establishment of one well-equipped and staffed Preventive Health Care (PHC) centre in each village. To increase the number of qualified medical personnel, the State would introduce a special three year medical course designed to produce qualified healthcare specialists in a shorter period of time.

Access to employment opportunities - The State would ensure the creation of employment opportunities for all. This would not be constrained by geographical, social or economic considerations.

> In order to realise the vision, the State has set for itself time bound goals viz. achieving 100 per cent literacy, increasing the irrigation potential by 200 per cent, connecting all villages with metalled roads, empowering women etc.

Reducing the population growth rate - During the last decade, Chhattisgarh has witnessed a lower decadal growth rate (1.86% per annum) than that of India as a whole. It plans to further reduce this growth rate to 1.48% per annum (Exhibit IV.2) for the period 2001-2010

Exhibit IV.2

Population Growth Rate (CAGR)

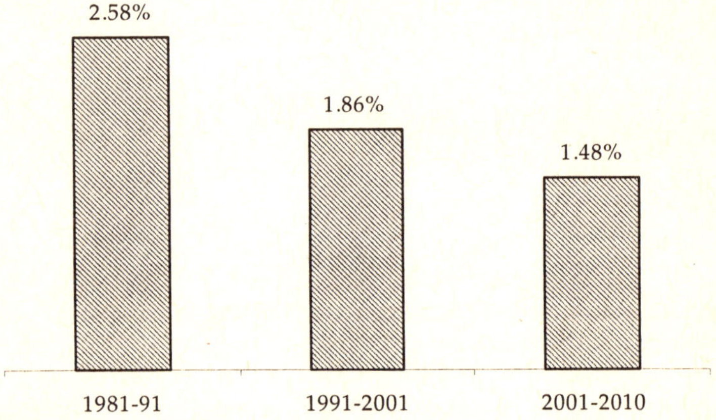

In order to meet the above targets, the government would work on revitalising the State's economy and strive to:

Double the Net State Domestic Product (NSDP) - The NSDP (at constant 1993-94 prices) would increase to Rs. 300,710 million by 2009-10 from the current Rs 153,710 (approx.) at a CAGR of 7.75% (Exhibit IV.3). This growth in NSDP would increase gradually from 4.2% in 2001-02 to 11.5% by the year 2009-10 in real terms.

Redefine sectoral composition of NSDP - All the three sectors would contribute to the envisaged growth in NSDP. However, in line with the longer term developmental priorities of the Vision, the sectoral composition of the economy would undergo changes (Exhibit IV.4 -5). At present, the major contributor to NSDP is the primary sector, accounting for 37% of the NSDP. However, by 2010 the tertiary sector would replace the primary sector as the major contributor to the economy and would account for 41% of NSDP

Exhibit IV.3

NSDP Growth Rate (CAGR)

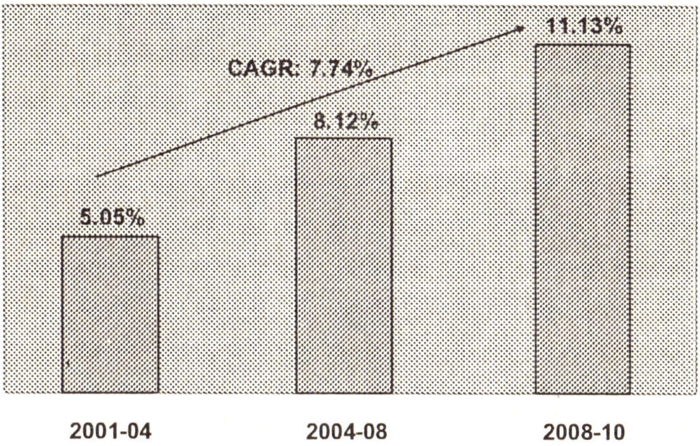

- **Primary sector** - The contribution of this sector to the NSDP is expected to decrease to about 31% by 2010. This however, does not imply that the thrust on this sector would reduce. It just implies that other sectors would grow at a higher rate over the next 10 years. The growth rate of the primary sector is expected to double in the first 5-6 years, during which time the State would follow a strategy of leveraging on its key strength - natural resources

- **Secondary sector** - By 2010, the contribution of the secondary sector to the economy is expected to remain at its current level. Growth in this sector is expected to be fuelled by the growth in the primary sector and through new investments in value added industries.

> By 2010, Chhattisgarh would double its NSDP from its current level and restructure the contribution of the primary, secondary and tertiary sector to sustain rapid growth in the future years.

- **Tertiary sector** - The tertiary sector comprises of transportation, trade, tourism, real estate, banking, recreation, amusement etc. The tertiary sector would grow in tandem

Exhibit IV.4

Sectoral Composition of NSDP

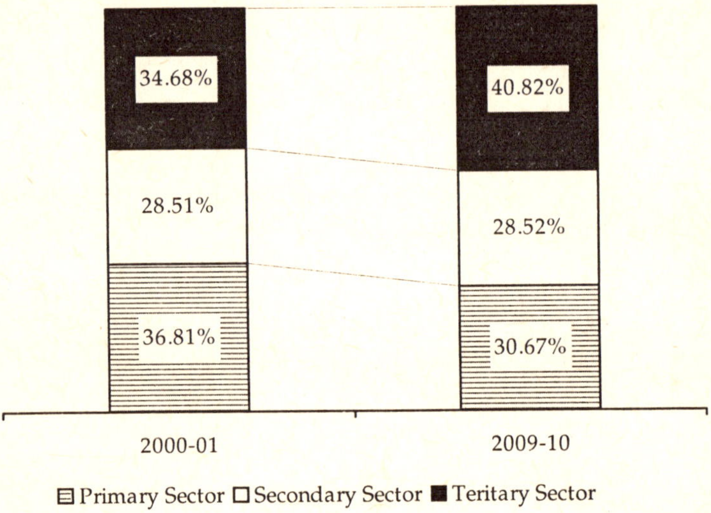

Exhibit IV.5

Sectoral Growth Rate (CAGR)

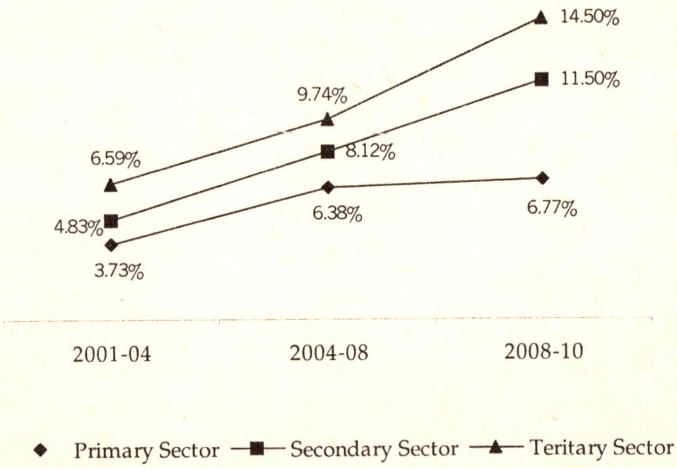

with the growth in the primary and secondary sectors in the initial years. But, this growth would increase significantly in the later years, by which time the State would have made considerably more progress in terms of building its physical infrastructure.

Increase the per capita income by over Rs.5000 - The per capita income would increase from the present value of Rs. 7,072 to Rs.12, 276 in 2010, growing at a CAGR of 6.17%. This is expected to increase over the years (Exhibit IV.6 -overleaf) as a result of the increase in the rate of growth of NSDP and a reduction in the rate of growth of population.

> Currently the major contributor to NSDP is the primary sector accounting for 37%. However, by 2010 the tertiary sector would replace the primary sector as the major contributor to the economy and would account for 41% of the NSDP

Exhibit IV.6

Per Capita Income (CAGR)

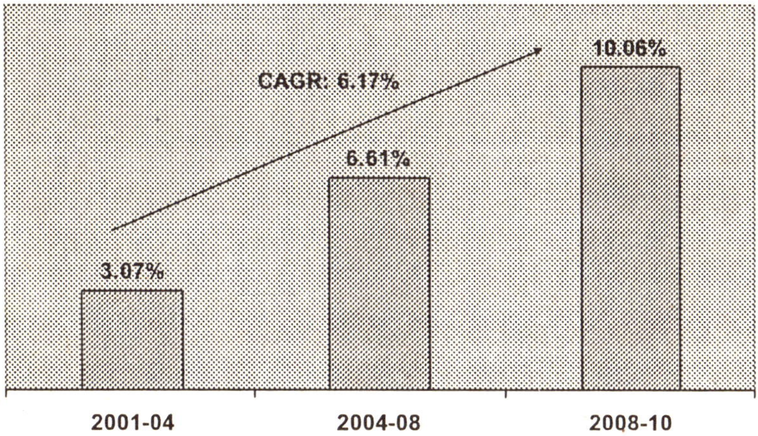

These measurable goals and targets set out above can only be achieved through a set of focussed strategies that involve the judicious use of natural assets along with substantial investments in physical and human infrastructure.

Jharkhand

Vision : 2010

Jharkhand: Vision 2010

INTRODUCTION

Jharkhand, India's 28th State, came into existence on 15th Nov. 2000. This State came into being with a commitment to an all-round development and prosperity of its people in general and scheduled tribes and scheduled castes in particular. Having lived amidst the nature, the people of Jharkhand understand the value and importance of sustainable development. This document sets out the vision and aspirations of the people of Jharkhand for achieving social equity, prosperity and involvement of the weakest and most backward sections of the society in the developmental process.

The Jharkhand State is located at latitudes 22°O' N to 24° 50' N and longitude 83° 20' E to 88° O'E and is bound by the States of Bihar on the North, West Bengal in the East, Orissa in the South and Uttar Pradesh in the West. The State is divided into 22 districts comprising 4 divisions. Covering an area of 79,714 Sq. Kms., it has 152 towns and 32,615 villages. The total population as per 2001 Census is 26.91 Million. The decadal (1991-2001) population growth rate was 23.19%, which is lower than the growth rate of Bihar (28.40%) but higher than the growth rate for the country as a whole (21.30%). The population density is 338 per Sq. Km. compared to the average population density of 324 for the country as a whole. The sex ratio of 934 is close to all India average (933) but is higher than that of Bihar (921). The literacy rate for Jharkhand is 54.13%, out of which male literacy rate is 67.94% and female literacy rate is 39.38%. More than one-fifth of the total population (22.3%) lives in urban areas indicating that Jharkhand has a higher degree of urbanization than Bihar (10.50%) but a lower level of urbanization than the all-India average of 27.8%. The State has five cities with a population of 1,00,000 and above. The cultivable area is 38 lakh Hectares and the present net sown area is 18.04 lakh Hectares. The net irrigated area is only 1.57 lakh Hectares, which is 8% of the total sown area.

Jharkhand is one of the richest states in the country in terms of mineral resources. Ironically, it is also one of the most backward regions of the country. The State is also endowed with a rich forest cover. About 29% of the total forest and recorded as forest land out of which only 19% is actually under forest cover. It has a vast potential for generating hydroelectric power.

The State and its Government are committed to accelerate the pace of development with a view to transform Jharkhand into a modern state. The development policy emphasizes the need for intensifying efforts to achieve development both in the economic and the social spheres so that state can realise its full economic potential and even the weakest and the most backward can become active participants in the development process.

High growth rates are possible through the development of the Industry & the Services sectors. These sectors, by virtue of being high value generators, provide higher gains on an average. In addition, through the creation of new job opportunities they ensure employment opportunities for betterment for the populace at large. Services sector, in particular, tends to be highly labour and skill intensive.

Agriculture, in contrast, tends to experience lower growth rates. It is also perhaps responsible for the wide fluctuations in the performance of the state. On the other hand, agriculture provides livelihood to the majority of the population. Therefore, robust and consistent growth in this sector is the best guarantee for achieving broad-based growth of incomes and employment levels, especially in the rural areas. More than 77% of the state population resides in rural areas and depends on agriculture for sustenance. In this scenario, the development of this sector becomes critical to the entire socio-economic developmental process of the State. Any developmental initiative is therefore incomplete without due consideration to this sector. Agricultural development is desirable not only for its direct impact on the lives of 70-80% of the population dependent on it, but also for its favourable impact on the other sectors of industry and services. Development of the rural non-farm sector (RNFS), which is equally important for its impact on the development process through employment creation, higher incomes and poverty alleviation is also dependent on a dynamic agricultural sector for its growth.

Poverty, which is largely concentrated in rural areas, can be effectively targeted through the generation of greater employment opportunities and improved returns. While the employment elasticity of agriculture may not be favourable, its allied sectors of Horticulture, Dairy, Fisheries etc. are highly labour intensive and offer huge employment potential. These sectors, Dairy and Inland Fisheries in particular, are not dependent on land and therefore constitute an effective means of targeting the land-less poor.

While economic growth and employment opportunities go a long way in improving the living conditions of the poor, they in themselves are not enough. They need to be combined with the provision of social infrastructure and services such as primary education and healthcare, safe drinking water, sanitation etc. Building capabilities in the weaker sections is an effective means of improving their access to opportunities and therefore prosperity.

There are regions or pockets of backwardness, predominantly tribal, which have remained isolated from the over-all growth process. Special attention needs to be focused on such regions to integrate them with the rest of the economy. The development of agriculture and other rural activities, through improvement in productivity and providing connectivity to these backward areas is a powerful tool for addressing regional disparities.

It is therefore obvious that all the three sectors of Agriculture, Industry & Services will have to be simultaneously targeted for the development of the state economy. While Agriculture will continue to be the mainstay of the economic process in the short to medium term, Industry & Services will take over and will start accruing benefits in the medium to long term.

Our vision for the State in the year 2010 is a Jharkhand free from poverty where every individual is able to lead a comfortable and healthy life. Where basic minimum needs of food, shelter, health, education, drinking water have been taken care of and each individual is able to access all the opportunities for his personal, educational and skill development. Where the environment is clean and the life and property of individuals is safe. A State where there is no hunger, exploitation, discrimination or deprivation. We are committed to achieve that.

Our Vision-2010 may be summarized as follows:-

1. The Gross Domestic Product of the State will grow at an average annual rate of 9 per cent with average growth rates for agriculture, industry and services sector being 5, 10 and 11 per cent respectively;
2. The poverty levels would have come down from 54 per cent at present to 35 per cent by 2010. Further, the gap between male and female wages would have been eliminated.
3. The State shall be sufficient in food production and would have fully utilized the potential of horticultural development. There will be adequate infrastructure for storage and preservation of agricultural produce.
4. Increase in irrigated area from 8 per cent to 25 per cent.
5. All the degraded forest will stand restored and the total forest cover would stand increased to 33 per cent of the total land area.
6. It will be ensured that the mineral wealth is not haphazardly exploited but developed in a sustainable manner consistent with the targeted levels of economic growth.
7. Jharkhand will have a strong and diversified industrial base capable of creating large-scale productive employment opportunities. The State shall also emerge as one of the most preferred destination for industrial investment in Asia.
8. The State shall ensure assured, uninterrupted and quality power supply to commercial and individual consumers and all the villages will be energized.
9. Connecting all district headquarters with State capital, inter connecting district and Block headquarters, strengthening

and double laning of all inter-state high-ways, connecting all tourist and religious places and connecting all villages through all weather roads.

10. All the citizens of Jharkhand will have safe, efficient, regular, comfortable and cost effective transport facilities. The vehicular pollution will be kept under control and an integrated transport systems both for passenger and goods will be in place.
11. All necessary physical infrastructure like water supply, sewerage and solid waste management, roads/bridges and environment improvement in urban areas will be developed to enable citizens to lead a healthy life in a clean environment.
12. All children will be in school by 2005 and all children would have completed 5 years of schooling by 2010.
13. The gender gaps in literacy will stand reduced by at least 75 per cent.
14. Increase in literacy rate from 54.13 per cent to 85 per cent.
15. Every individual in the State will have free access to primary healthcare.
16. The State shall ensure the availability of secondary and tertiary healthcare at affordable costs.
17. The endemic diseases like TB and Malaria etc. would have been eradicated.
18. Reduction of Infant mortality rate (IMR) from 72 (1998) to 40 per 1000 live births.
19. Reduction of Maternal mortality ratio (MMR) from 4 (1998) to 1 per 1000 live births.
20. Universal immunisation coverage for pregnant mothers and infants.
21. All villages will have sustained access to potable drinking water and environment sanitation.
22. Sustainable socio-economic development of the Scheduled Tribes including primitive tribals groups (PTG), Scheduled Castes and other backward classes.

23. Reduction in incidence of poverty afflicting the rural masses by 20 per cent, providing gainful employment along with ensuring availability of food grains through the mechanism of wages in kind and providing shelter for the homeless.

24. Sufficient and efficient food storage capacity up to village level and a responsive distribution infrastructure owned and operated by the community will be in place. This will ensure complete food security to the people, especially those who are economically marginalized.

25. Providing a simple, efficient, transparent, accountable government to the people of the state. The Government will also to work as a catalytic agent for a holistic and sustainable development. Empowering the people through the growth of Panchayati Raj and Municipal institutions.
    - Strengthening institutional framework to render science and technology (S&T) accessible to the people.
    - Creating scientific aptitude and temperament in the masses to remove various myths and practices in the society through information technology.
    - Creating conducive scientific environment for real governance for providing transparent, smart, paperless and quick service to the masses.
    - Developing IT and bio-technology skills in the State.

26. The tourism sector will be developed as state priority in a sustainable manner, so that it contributes to the improvement in the quality of life of our people. The manifold tourism related resources of the State would be utilized optimally in an eco-friendly manner thereby developing Jharkhand into an up market high quality tourist destination.

27. Eliminating all forms of exploitation of the labour force and to actively protect interest of labourers specially in unorganised sectors. Eliminating gender gap in wage rates.

Vision 2020 CD

Registration Form for FREE CD

Please note that we have also brought a companian CD to the book Vision 2020. This CD contains the following vision documents (Complete)

Andhra Pradesh Vision 2020

Chhattisgarh Vision 2010

Assam Vision 2025

Jharkhand Vision 2010

In order to avail the free CD, kindly provide us the following information.

Name ....

Designation ....

Organisation ....

Address ....

....

City ....

Pin ....

State ....

Phone ....

E-Mail ....

Fax ....

Book was purchased from ....

(Name & city of the selling agent / bookshop)

Kindly attach a Draft or Delhi payable Cheque favouring ACADEMIC FOUNDATION TRP amounting Rs. 75/- towards postage and handling charges for the CD. The charges will not be applicable in case of CD being collected from our office.

NOTE: This offer is valid only for the end user. This CD will be made available directly from Academic Foundation only and not from the bookshop from where the book has been purchased. The form is to be submitted in original. No photocopy will be entertained.

This form is to be sent to:

Academic Foundation
4772-73/23, Bharat Ram Road,
(23, Ansari Road), Daryaganj, New Delhi - 110002.
Ph: 23245001, 02, 03, 04 Fax: 23245005

Cut along this line